Acclaim for

MICHAEL ERIC DYSON

and **RACE RULES**

"A lively, eclectic, and plainspoken critic. . . . Like every great teacher, Dyson is remarkable for his belief that those of us he is preaching to really can change for the better."
                                                            —*Elle*

"Strong, timely and important . . . often brilliant and always electric in its energy. . . . A warm, intelligent, often deliciously amusing work that lets nobody—including its own author—off the hook."
                    —Jonathan Kozol, author of *Amazing Grace*

"In *Race Rules*, Michael Eric Dyson lights a fire as he challenges and probes even the most sacred of our thoughts and attitudes. Ultimately, that fire warms your spirit, rekindles your faith, and offers a light of hope."
                    —Iyanla Vanzant, author of *Acts of Faith*
                                           and *Spirit of Man*

"Penetrating. . . . Dyson delivers some sound, well-grounded analyses."   —*Emerge*

"Brilliant. . . . Written with the ease of a good novel, this is a book that everyone who cares about the future of our country must read."   —E. Lynn Harris, author of
                                           And This Too Shall Pass

MICHAEL ERIC DYSON

RACE RULES

Michael Eric Dyson is the author of *Making Malcolm: The Myth and Meaning of Malcolm X* and, most recently, *Between God and Gangsta Rap: Bearing Witness to Black Culture*. His writing has also appeared in *The New York Times*, *The New York Times Book Review*, *Washington Post Book World*, *The Nation*, *Chicago Tribune*, *Vibe*, *Emerge*, and *Rolling Stone*. He is a Distinguished Visiting Professor at Columbia's Institute for Research in African American Studies.

Also by

MICHAEL ERIC DYSON

Between God and Gangsta Rap:
Bearing Witness to Black Culture

Making Malcolm:
The Myth and Meaning of Malcolm X

Reflecting Black:
African-American Cultural Criticism

RACE RULES

MICHAEL ERIC DYSON

RACE RULES

NAVIGATING THE COLOR LINE

VINTAGE BOOKS

A Division of Random House, Inc.   New York

FIRST VINTAGE BOOKS EDITION, SEPTEMBER 1997

Library of Congress Cataloging-in-Publication Data
Dyson, Michael Eric.
Race rules : navigating the color line / Michael Eric Dyson.
p.   cm.
ISBN 0-679-78156-0
1. United States—Race relations. 2. Afro-Americans—Social conditions—1975-
I. Title.
[E185.615.D95   1997]
305.8'00973—dc21   97-5433
CIP

TO MY BROTHERS

Anthony Dyson
Gregory Dyson
Brian Dyson
for your companionship and support along the way

AND ESPECIALLY TO

Everett Dyson-Bey
Prisoner #212687
for his determination to free his body and mind
and for his heroic will to survive the madness of his fate

Contents

CONTENTS

RACE RULES

RACE RULES

Race Plus Rage Equals Ruin

Race Rules

In this case, the danger, in the minds of most white Americans, is the loss of their identity. Try to imagine how you would feel if you woke up one morning to find the sun shining and all the stars aflame. You would be frightened because it is out of the order of nature. Any upheaval in the universe is terrifying because it so profoundly attacks one's sense of one's own reality. Well, the black man has functioned in the white man's world as a fixed star, as an immovable pillar: and as he moves out of his place, heaven and earth are shaken to their foundations.

James Baldwin
The Fire Next Time, 1963

WHY ANOTHER BOOK ON RACE? Let me tell you a story.

It was a beautiful day in Chapel Hill. I'd just returned from a book and lecture tour that had taken me across America. Along the way, I'd made appearances on several national television programs. As I discussed my book on these shows, the themes that I had written about—black masculinity, the politics of race, contemporary black music— were very much in the news. Hip-hop was under attack, and I talked about that. Black men were serving longer jail sentences for abusing crack cocaine than their white counterparts were serving for abusing powdered cocaine. I talked about that. The Million Man March dominated the news for a while. I talked about that. I also talked about black preachers, soul music, Shakespeare and Smokey Robinson, Marion Barry, Sam Cooke, Michael Jordan, and about most everything that touched on contemporary black culture. And of course, inevitably, I talked about O.J.

Now, after my return to North Carolina, I went into my office to retrieve my mail. Predictably, it was stacked high. Besides bills, ads for books, and the usual stuff academics get, the pile contained a bunch of letters. Because of the subjects about which I write, speak, lecture, and preach, people write me a lot. I riffled through the letters, setting this one aside until much later, putting this one aside to read that evening because something about it was compelling, and so on. But one letter stood out. It demanded to be read right away. And so I read it.

The writer was obviously a man. A white man. A white man of high intelligence. A white man of high intelligence who was full of rage. That can be a dangerous combination.

His rage spilled out on every page of his eloquent, sarcastic, witty, biting missive. He had obviously found out that I was on leave for the semester, and he pointed to this as proof that I am a privileged professor (which I am) at a prestigious southern university (which it is). My privilege, and the prestige of my surroundings, should have prevented my "gall to talk about the white community in this country inhibiting black opportunity." I didn't remember saying that about all whites, but I conceded him the point for argument's sake. Opportunity is everywhere, he wrote. But black folk must take advantage. Especially since black students are being sought by major academic institutions. But why don't blacks take advantage of these opportunities? "There aren't enough quality black students." Why? "Because the black family unit in this country has fallen apart."

Throughout his letter, the writer seems to think that I blame white folk for everything that's wrong with black folk. Of course, that's a position I've argued against in my work. But if I had come across to him that way, I was glad to know it. Who knows, he might be speaking for millions of whites who feel the same way. "You cannot blame white America for the black family. At some point, you must begin to accept responsibility for what you have done," he writes. Well, yes, of course. That's why a few brothers (of which I was one) held a little gathering called the Million Man March. But the writer's rage, I think, will not be satisfied by such meager gestures.

"I've seen the pocket of ignorance which sits at the *core* of the black experience in America," he opines. (Whew! That's awful harsh. At the core of the black experience? Not much hope, huh?) "It's a sight most Americans see only fleetingly on TV, and one which black leaders and scholars don't talk about much. This is a huge lump of despair. Inert and incorrigible. This is the problem."

Well, it's part of the problem, at least. And it is difficult to talk about on TV, where substance is sometimes sacrificed for style. But a lot of black scholars and intellectuals have talked about the despair, and other problems, in black America. I didn't expect the writer to know about it because a lot of that work gets ignored, especially in white communities. So I pressed on.

The writer tells of his experience as a teacher for a year in Watts in 1984. To be brief, the black kids don't come off too well. They don't watch PBS, C-SPAN, or CNN. "They're tuned to sports, rap music, and the like. Who do you wanna blame for that?" Black parents fare no better. Their parenting skills are zilch. They won't even watch programs on TV about parenting. "But those young mothers are watching soap operas and trash talk shows. As for reading a book on the subject, forget about it, most can't read." My writer talks about the tribal conflicts in Africa, which are surely, he says, "a form of racism." Alas, he queries, "Who would you blame for African tribalism/racism?"

Indeed, my writer says that he's known a lot more black racists than white racists in this country. Then he makes a remarkable statement: "In all sincerity, race isn't much of an issue for mainstream white America. We're busy. It's a complicated world. We have bigger problems to deal with. We're too preoccupied with simple survival to go around organizing systematic prejudice of any kind."

Say what? I read that line over and over again. I was hunting for the deeper meaning. After all, my correspondent was obviously a smart guy, and, despite his rage, I didn't think he was, by any means, an evil person.

But then I thought, I can see how "race isn't much of an issue for mainstream white America," because their lives aren't at stake the same way black lives are. Their lives aren't haunted and torn by race's complex, twisted meanings. That is, not until O.J. That's when a lot of white folk felt the crunch, the collective sense of denied justice that black folk breathe like the air. O.J. put an end to all that unconsciousness about race, that taking for granted the safe boundaries between white and black experiences. He ripped the facade right off our social relations. O.J. was, in fact, the reason my writer had written to me in the first place.

For my writer, O.J. was "the ultimate example of black success in America." He was "this colorless pitchman, this poor, black kid who became a rich, raceless, world citizen." True for most of that. He certainly tried to become colorless and raceless. But as the trial proved, he wasn't quite the success he was cracked up to be. My letter writer goes on to say O.J. was a womanizer. True. A wife beater. True. And that we all know, that I know, that O.J. killed his wife. Well, I don't know that everybody believes that. Not even all white people believe that.

My writer claims Johnnie Cochran "sold that jury, his own people, out. He knows O.J. did it...And for a few bucks and a hollow, pyrrhic victory, he made that jury look like a bunch of idiots to the overwhelming majority of the population of this country. He connected with them at a level of tribal, black, superstitious, jive, stupidity that was frightening. America saw what the black community was really made of, and it was a sickening sight." Damn! But then, this is how a lot of black folk believe white folk felt about us way before the O.J. trial. The verdicts were a convenient excuse to express what was always there.

My writer offers that people "who maintain his innocence typically don't know the facts, have not dared to confront the facts of the case. Are not educated." Wow! A whole lot of highly intelligent, well read, black and white folk I know, who followed the trial closely—including some lawyers—thought that O.J. should be found not guilty.

My writer's rage now explodes. The black jury showed white America "what all the legislation, all the Affirmative Action, all the billions of welfare dollars had bought over the past three decades: a cloying ignorance now empowered." Now that's pretty tough. Maybe even mean-spirited and spiteful. But there's more. "That [cloying ignorance now empowered] is the issue, and this is your problem. Because in millions of conversations each day, all across this country, white people are asking themselves, why feel guilty? We've done our part. And look what these black people do. And so it now becomes a lot easier to vote Affirmative Action out, to pull back on welfare, and to insist that black people take responsibility for their own actions, just like all other Americans."

Man! You mean white folk are ready to do all that because of the O.J. verdicts? Acquitting O.J. is the greatest symbol ever of black ingratitude—that's really the subtext here— beyond whatever else black folk might have done to offend white folk? Beyond the 1992 LA riots? Beyond Colin Ferguson's demented demonstration of black hatred and rage? Beyond *anything* we've ever done? O.J.?

And where has our writer been? What about all the black leaders, from Booker T. Washington to Jesse Jackson and, yes, even Louis Farrakhan, who have preached about black folk taking responsibility for their own lives? Of course, the more insightful black leaders have always understood that responsibility is a complex, dynamic affair. It's not just about the choices folk make. It's also about the choices they have available to them. But I'm getting ahead of the story.

Our writer believes that black people "have used blackness as an excuse for failure way too long. It's become a crutch." (Remember Jesse Jackson saying, "My people, let Pharaoh go."?) But of the many other things he writes, one paragraph reveals the depth of his rage, a rage that is truly alarming.

My writer tells me of how the O.J. verdicts have transformed him: "Give you an example of how I've changed. Shortly after the O.J. verdict, there was a door slam and a scream in the hallway of my upscale Los Angeles apartment building. I opened my door to see what was the matter, baseball bat in hand, and found a young black woman, hysterical, complaining that she'd come out from Wisconsin to visit my neighbor, a Japanese student I didn't know, and he was abusing her. I grew up in Wisconsin and could imagine how confusing and frightening LA was for her. Prior to the verdict I'd have said yes to her request to enter my apartment to use the phone. But I thought to myself, when the wife-abuser-beater-murderer was let go I bet she was jumping up and down celebrating the verdict with the rest of black America. And I turned my back on her, and closed my door. Let her work it out."

Well, there's more. But that's enough. My writer is, I believe, not atypical of many white folk who watched O.J. and lost it. All their reserve. All their finesse. All their genuine effort to make things better (my writer said that he had worked for equality all his life, and I believe him). All the good will. All of it, gone. Out the window. How could such an intelligent man, a thoughtful man, come to such bitter, rage-filled, sometimes mean-spirited conclusions? Is there any hope for Americans to bridge the gap between whites and blacks? Not to mention the incredible zones of ethnic difference represented by Asian, Latino, Native American, and other minority communities.

Why another book on race? The answer is simple. Because we haven't learned our lessons. We still don't know the *rules of race*. Of course, there are many more than I can

cover here. But we've got to begin somewhere. I'm not referring only to rules that address interaction *between* the
races, which, given recent events, are certainly important to
learn. There is a need to explore as well the *rules of the
race,* the unwritten codes of conduct *within* black communities. After all, as Ralph Ellison pointed out, black folk
couldn't "live and develop for over three hundred years
simply by *reacting*" to the white majority.

As I've traveled around the nation, I've encountered
forms of black disgust—perhaps even of rage, paralleling my
correspondent's rage—with aspects of black culture. Older
folk are disgusted with youth. A lot of intellectuals are mad
at the few media darlings who've been crowned Voice of
the Négro. Many black Christians are hurting, bruised by the
sexual hypocrisy that mars the black church's great legacy
of liberation. There's a fair bit of anger at the failures of black
leadership. And there's a great deal of black female anger at
what women see as the disgusting, confusing behavior of
black men, while many brothers are fed up with what they
perceive as the insensitive, uncomprehending perspectives
of black women. A lot of poor folk feel betrayed by the
well-to-do, many of whom, in turn, are contemptuous of
black street culture. I'd like to help us to begin the process
of open, honest communication about the differences
within our race. So I'm interested in those forms of racial
etiquette—those rules—that are being observed and broken, often without honest, clear communication between
hurt parties.

The rules I have in mind, the ones I explore here, are not
prescriptive. Rather, they describe the sorts of thinking and
behavior that I see operating among and between blacks
and whites. I'd like to help us navigate the issues of power,
justice, and equality that divide blacks and whites, and that

echo in black communities as well. As I think about it, I am also examining how race rules in the varied contexts of my life: as a black American, a black intellectual, a black preacher, a black father, a black citizen, and a black man.

The real arguments for these rules rest in the details, in the careful reflection on race I hope to offer in these pages. And I think it's necessary to always link the rules of the race to the rules of race. Ellison is certainly right that black culture isn't a mere record of reaction to white life. But it has certainly been, and continues to be, shaped by white life. And, as Ellison understood, black culture shapes white life as well.

The writer of the letter warned me that "it's the duty of educated, successful academics like you to dispel this notion of misplaced blame." The blame he had in mind was how black folk blame white folk for our problems. A lot of black folk, indeed most black folk I know, don't, refuse to, can't blame white folk for our problems. But these black folk know that the demand for racial justice is not the same as blaming white folk for our problems. Rather it is insisting that our nation take seriously the lesson it tries to teach black folk: Take responsibility for what you've done!

My writer's letter—plus the rage that black folk express to and for one another—is why I've written this book. I want to speak to, and about, the pain and rage that fester inside that man, inside all of us. Inside our entire country. Race continues to plague our lives. Race continues to make a difference. Race continues to dominate. Race rules.

ONE

When You're a Credit to Your Race, the Bill Will Come Due

O.J. Simpson and Our Trial by Fire

> *Now it says here, "And every white man shall be allowed to pet himself a Negro. Yea, he shall take a black man unto himself to pet and to cherish, and this same Negro shall be perfect in his sight...." The appointer has his reasons, personal or political. He can always point to the beneficiary and say, "Look, Negroes, you have been taken care of. Didn't I give a member of your group a big job?".*
>
> Zora Neale Hurston
> "The 'Pet' Negro System," 1943

THE STUDIO CRACKLED WITH EXCITEMENT. Although I had appeared on Black Entertainment Television (BET) a few times before, this night was special. In fact, it was extraordinary. Former BET anchor Ed Gordon, my Detroit homeboy, had snagged the first televised interview with O.J. Simpson since his acquittal for the murder of his ex-wife, Nicole, and her companion, Ron Goldman. BET asked me to give "color commentary" before and after Simpson's appearance. A large irony, indeed. I'd written about Simpson in my previous book, and I'd discussed his trial on other national television shows. But there was poetic justice in me talking about Simpson's trials and tribulations, and those of black America, on the only television station that caters to black folk.

I must confess that I was an O.J. addict. I watched the trial every day for hours at a time. I was completely mesmerized. I knew it was a vulgar display of American excess. I knew it was the revelation of the gaudiness behind the lifestyles of the rich and famous. (Of course, I took delight in seeing so many rich folk exposed for the shallow people many of us hoped they'd be.) I knew it was the theater of the absurd meets the Twilight Zone. I knew as well that the trial was a painful choreography of black grief—that of O.J. and of every black person who identified with him—before an international audience. I knew it was totally artificial, a sordid drama full of kitsch that fiendishly aspired to the status of morality play. I knew it was the story of a black man who had made good but who had forgotten what made it possible, which made it bad. I knew it was all that and much, much more. And I couldn't stop watching.

Even as questions about O.J.'s guilt or innocence fade from daily debate, we continue to grapple with the wounds the trial exposed, with the trial's revelations of the pernicious rules of race in America, '90s style. That night, as I viewed Simpson on the big screen in BET's green room, I was struck again by how flawless his face is, how smooth his skin is. But I was taken as well by the jagged horrors his eyes never gaze on—how many white folk now hate his name, how they wish he would disappear. And some wish him dead. And how black folk look at him with a mix of pity and disdain. Like the member of the family you have to recognize but hate to, because the recognition embarrasses him as well. I was struck by the size of the denials by which Simpson lives, as if he must now draw energy from the resentment that he can't afford to acknowledge, though its sheer vehemence defines and confirms his every step. Seeing Simpson so resiliently spiteful that night—not in any way bitter against whites, just against the idea that they might not love him—made it painful for me to have to say anything after he spoke. It was the final step in my loss of a hero who had once thrilled me, as he, in Ralph Ellison's words, "slice[d] through an opposing line with a dancer's slithering grace." A part of me was now gone. It was sad, and sadly disorienting.

Something of the same disorientation gripped America when Simpson was set free. When the not guilty verdicts in the O.J. Simpson double-murder case were handed down, the compass of race went haywire. The Simpson case has made many Americans doubt if we can all get along. The case has rudely reminded us of a gigantic and numbing racial divide. It reminds us, too, that boasting about racial progress often hides racial pain. The response to the verdicts knocked down the floodgates that hold back the waters of racial hostility. The Simpson case also taught us a tough lesson: the more settled race relations seem to be, the more likely they are raging beneath the surface.

Americans have become addicted to the Simpson case for more than its grotesque exaggeration of our secret racial fears. From its very beginning the case was overloaded with huge social meanings we claim not to be able to understand under normal circumstances. We have become dependent on the Simpson case to represent complicated truths that we think can only be illustrated by catastrophe. That dependence shows contempt for ordinary signs of ruin. It ignores the experience of common people, especially blacks, whose silent suffering is the most powerful evidence of decay. What their experience shows us is this: a two-tiered universe of perception rotates around an axis defined by race. While good fortune lights one side, despair darkens the other. It is rarely sunny at the same time in white and black America. In a nutshell, that's what the Simpson case reminds us of.

That O.J. Simpson is at the heart of the most ugly racial spectacle to hit America in decades is a symptom of just how crazy things are. For a quarter century, Simpson symbolized the icon-next-door. His athletic genius was revered by many blacks. His athletic skill and "colorless" image were attractive to millions of whites.

Simpson's sleek form and catlike grace as a running back brought glamor to a brutal sport. Simpson beautifully combined judgment and intuition. His sixth sense for where his pursuers were likely to pounce on him allowed him to chisel arteries of escape around heaving bodies.

As with many famous athletes, Simpson's athletic exploits gave him influence beyond the boundaries of his sport. This is hardly natural. After all, why should athletes receive tons of money and notoriety beyond the recognition and compensation they earn in sports? The absurdity of this is masked by the fact that we take for granted that such things should occur. That's not to say sports don't teach us valuable lessons about life. Sports are often a powerful training ground for moral excellence. Take the case of Willis Reed, the injured center for the 1969–70 New York Knicks who was not expected to play in the seventh and deciding game for the NBA championship. When Reed emerged from the locker room, limping but determined to compete, several virtues were literally embodied: sacrifice of self for the sake of the larger good; the courage to "play through pain"; and the sort of moral leadership that rallies one's teammates and lifts their level of expectation and achievement. These virtues transcend sport. They inspire ordinary people to overcome obstacles in achieving their goals.

There's another way, one wholly beyond his choosing, that the rare athlete has managed to rise beyond the limits of his sport. Some figures have served as heroic symbols of national identity. Others have heroically represented achievement against the artificial restrictions imposed on a group of people. In those cases, a restriction was also placed on competition as an ideal of democratic participation. Joe DiMaggio, of course, fit the first bill. His 56-game hitting streak in baseball thrilled America in 1941, a colossal feat of endurance to which the nation would turn its attention time and again as our preeminence as a world power began to fade after World War II. Jackie Robinson fit the second meaning of heroism. As major league baseball's first black player, Robinson performed gallantly in the face of bitter opposition. His gifted play paved the way for blacks in his sport and beyond the bounds of baseball.

Joe Louis managed the difficult art of fulfilling both sorts of heroism. He existed in a racial era just as complex—if more violent—as the one Robinson faced. As was true of DiMaggio's Italian world, Louis's black community celebrated its ethnic roots while affirming its American identity. Louis captured the genius of American citizenship and the protest of blacks against their exclusion from full citizenship in a single gesture: the punch that sunk German boxer Max Schmeling at the height of Nazism. That punch transformed Louis into an American hero. It also revealed the hidden meaning of Louis's heroic art: beating white men in the ring was a substitute argument for social equality. Louis's prizefighting was an eloquent plea to play the game of American citizenship by one set of rules.

Simpson never aspired to that sort of heroism. In part, that's because the times didn't demand it. Near the start of Simpson's pro career in the late '60s, the tension between the older civil rights establishment and the newer black power movement produced a more acerbic model of black heroism. Instead of integration, many blacks preferred separating from white society to build black institutions. Black antiheroism gave an angry face to the resentment that festered in pockets of black life. To be an American and a Negro—later still, a black man—were not considered flip sides of the same coin. They were different currency altogether.

Judging from Simpson's behavior during the height of his career, he had no interest in claiming whatever remained of Louis's heroic inheritance. Neither was Simpson attracted to the sort of antiheroism championed by his contemporary, Muhammad Ali. Ali's self-promoting verse and brilliant boxing proved to be sparring matches for his real battle: the defiance of white authority because of his religious beliefs. And Simpson certainly wasn't drawn to the plainspoken demeanor of fellow athlete-turned-actor Jim Brown. Brown's militant, studly image had Crazy Negro written all over it. It was the opposite of everything Simpson seemed to stand for. That is, until he was charged with brutally slashing his ex-wife and her companion.

Simpson's appeal beyond sports rested on two related but distinct factors: commerce and the conscious crafting of a whitened image. Simpson came at the beginning of an era when athletes began to make enormous sums of money inside sports. (To be sure, Simpson's highest salary was pittance compared to what even mediocre sports figures now make.) He also helped pioneer the entrepreneurial athlete. Simpson hawked everything from tennis shoes to soft drinks. He turned charisma into cash on television. Now that Michael Jordan has eclipsed everyone who came before him, it's easy to forget that Simpson's Hertz commercials used to be the star athletes aimed for in marketing their fame.

The wide adulation heaped on Simpson beyond his gridiron glory also owed much to his absent, indeed *anti*-racial politics. Simpson soothed white anxieties about the racial turmoil caused by black radicalism. Simpson's Teflon racelessness assured white citizens and corporations that no negative, that is, exclusively black, racial inference would stick to his image. That is Jordan's charm as well. He is a latter-day Simpson of sorts. His universal appeal derives from a similar avoidance of the entanglements of race. As the old black saying goes, it's alright to *look* black, just don't *act* your color. As Simpson's case suggests, the Faustian bargain of trading color for commercial success may prove devastating in the long run.

Simpson's silence about race didn't necessarily have to be a bad thing. After all, given the history of their relative powerlessness, blacks have a heroic tradition of fighting in ways that cloak their rebellion. They adapt their speech and activity to the language and styles of the dominant society.

Silence in the presence of whites was often a crucial weapon in the war to survive. If it looked like blacks were happy to be oppressed, all the better. Such appearances greased the track of covert action on which black freedom rolled. For instance, slaves sang spirituals both to entertain their masters and to send each other coded messages about plans of escape.

Still, Simpson's privileged perch in white America led many blacks to hope that he might cautiously speak about the troubles of ordinary blacks. It soon became clear, however, that Simpson was having none of that. What many blacks wanted from Simpson was no different from what was expected of other blacks. Simpson was not expected to be a politician. At least not in any way that departed from the political behavior required of all blacks in O.J.'s youth, who had to carry themselves with an acute awareness of their surroundings. To do less meant early death. Or, more crushing, it meant a slow, painful surrender of life in gasps of frustrated energy because you just didn't understand the rules of survival in a white world.

IT'S EASY TO UNDERSTAND how O.J. and other blacks wanted to escape the demands of being representatives of The Race, its shining symbols. Standing in for the group was a burden. It was also risky. You could never be sure that your efforts were taken seriously. In fact, a law of inversion seemed to apply. For most blacks, only the negative acts seemed to count. Even the positive became a negative good: it only counted as a credit against black liability, against all the wrong things black folk inevitably did. The good you did simply meant that you, and, by extension, all blacks, didn't mess up this time. When the good was allowed to count, it only underscored one's uniqueness, that one was not like other black folk. For many whites, excellence made blacks exceptions to, not examples of, their race. Ironically, to be thought of as an exception to the race still denied a pure consideration of individual merit. As long as race colored the yardstick, a real measurement of individual achievement was impossible. It is a bitter paradox that the evaluation of individual achievement that blacks yearned for was subordinated to a consideration of any achievement's impact on, and relation to, the race. Blacks were routinely denied the recognition of individual talent that is supposed to define the American creed. This history is barely mentioned now that blacks are made by many whites to look as if they duck individual assessment while embracing group privilege.

The problem of representing The Race is compounded by whites who protest its injustice to famous blacks. "Why should they be made to represent the race?," well-meaning whites ask, as if anonymous blacks had more choice in the matter than their well-known peers. (Besides, such protest releases these whites from the awful burden of confronting racism in their own world. If the representative of The Race is relieved of duty, everybody can party. It also obscures how the need for racial representation was created by white racism to begin with.) The assumption is that fame makes the burden of representation heavier for some blacks. In many ways, that's true. There's more territory to cover. And there are certainly more folk to deal with in countering or confirming destructive views of black life. On the other hand, visible blacks have routes of escape that ordinary blacks will never know. The well-known black can bask in fortunes of fate most blacks will never be tempted by. They can make lots of money, join elite social clubs, live in exclusive neighborhoods, send their kids to tony schools, enjoy the lifestyles of the rich and famous. Famous blacks can cash

in on their complaints about having to repres
They can enjoy the fruits of a situation cre
being black in the first place.

Simpson took the path of least resistance fo
ing to dodge the burden of being black: ign
Although ignoring race is often mistaken for self-hatred,
they are not the same. Those who confuse them commit
what philosophers call a "category mistake." In such cases,
shades of meaning slip off the edges of sloppy distinctions.
Those who ignore race, and those who hate themselves
because they can't, do share self-defeating habits: both deny
the differences race makes and the lingering effects of
racism. But not all blacks who have these habits hate themselves or consciously set out to ignore race. Some blacks are
simply nonconformists who seek to defy the bitter boundaries of race, both within and beyond black life.

Simpson has confessed (not exactly, I'm afraid, what millions of Americans were hoping for) that it wasn't until he
got hate mail in jail that he admitted racism hadn't gone
away. Simpson concedes that he simply ignored or denied
racism for most of his adult life. Simpson's denial, combined
with his raceless image, entitled him to a derisive honor:
White Man's Negro. Simpson earned his crown by avoiding
and forgetting about race. He kept it by lusting after white
acceptance at any cost. On the face of it—at least the side of
his face he showed on the BET interview—that lust continues to shape his sense of reality. On the BET interview,
Simpson said most whites don't believe he's guilty. That
suggests more than Simpson's delusional state of mind. It
shows how his perception of events squares with the logic
of denial that made him useful to the white world. It is a
vicious twist of fate for Simpson. The same technique of survival that brought him praise from whites in the past—as he

as lauded, no doubt, for bravely resisting the demagogic demand to represent The Race—now causes those same whites to view him as pathological. No wonder O.J. is confused.

Simpson has now been forced to claim his race by default. It is an act that undoubtedly fills him—at least it would the old Simpson—with great regret. And not a little disdain. The blackness Simpson embraced during the trial was foreign to him. Its unfamiliar feel made him clutch it with great desperation. That blackness was molded for Simpson by Johnnie Cochran, who proved to be a shrewd conjurer of a "one size fits all" blackness. After all, it might complicate matters to acknowledge the conflicting varieties of black identity. In Cochran's conjuring, the complexity of race was skillfully shifted to a more narrow, but, on the surface at least, universal meaning of blackness-as-oppression. When applied to Simpson, such a meaning was laughable. It fit him even worse than the gloves prosecutor Christopher Darden tried to make Simpson force over his arthritic joints. But because blackness-as-oppression is often true for most blacks, Simpson benefited from its link to his case.

Darden, on the other hand, was unfairly stigmatized by Cochran's conjuring of blackness during the trial. Darden was viewed by many blacks as a traitor because he dared to call narrow blackness a phony idea in full view of white America. Darden failed because he didn't have Cochran's oratorical or lawyerly skills. (But Darden also had the thankless task of prosecuting a beloved, fallen American hero who was, at the same time, seeking to make a comeback to his black roots. Black folk are too often suckers for this sort of figure. Although blacks resent racial infidelity, we are often open to reconciliation. Even if the forgiven black continues to abuse the privilege of return, as Simpson has done.

It's painfully clear that black folk are his fallback, not his first choice.) Darden also goofed when he argued that black jurors would be outdone if they had to hear the dreaded "N" word, particularly if it leapt from the past of star prosecution witness, police detective Mark Fuhrman. Black folk endure that epithet and much worse every day.

Darden's naiveté and strategic mistakes made it easy to believe that he had little understanding of the harsh realities black folk routinely face. Ironically, Darden desperately tried to point out that it was Simpson who had avoided the hardship most blacks confront. In the symbolic war of blackness being waged between Darden and Cochran, Darden tried to make Simpson appear unworthy of the knee-jerk black loyalty he enjoyed but from which Darden had been excluded. But that point was skillfully shredded in rhetorical and legal crossfire with Cochran, both in the courtroom and in the court of public opinion.

Simpson *has* largely sidestepped the indignities imposed on ordinary blacks. His fame and fortune certainly helped. Equally important, Simpson has made a career out of making white folk feel safe. He has been an emissary of blackness-as-blandness. With O.J. present, there was no threat of black rage careening out of control. He made no unreasonable demands—or any reasonable ones for that matter—for change of any sort. He blessed the civility and rightness of the status quo. Indeed, O.J. got a big bonus by comparing favorably not only to black "hotheads," but to figures like Hank Aaron, the baseball legend whose mellow thunder led him to speak gently but insistently about racism in sports. Once Simpson put away his youthful law-breaking in San Francisco's Potrero Hill projects, he adopted a winning formula: he would play by the rules within the limits of the Given. The Given amounts to whites being on top. To win, you must act and talk white. In many interviews, Simpson has literally said so.

The extraordinary white hostility aimed at Simpson after the verdicts can largely be explained by the equally extraordinary investment O.J. made in the white world. He was a Good Negro who played by the rules. Many whites returned the favor. They invested in Simpson as a surrogate white. That investment explains their sense of betrayal by O.J. once he was charged, then cleared, of murder. According to the rules of surrogate whiteness, Simpson should have confessed his guilt and taken his punishment like a (white) man. Of course, by breaking the rules of surrogate whiteness, Simpson actually followed the rules of the Given: Those on top—wealthy whites—are not accountable to the system of justice in the same way as those on the bottom. The rules—of justice, fairness, equality—work fine for privileged whites as long as they are applied to a world of experience whites are familiar with. Beyond that territory, their sense of how and when the rules should apply is severely limited. That's the supreme paradox of white power Simpson learned up close.

It's not that white people are inherently more unfair or unjust than others. It's just that the rules are often applied in an arbitrary fashion to those outside the realm of their understanding and sympathy. That's why the barbarity of police brutality against blacks didn't faze many whites until the Rodney King beating and the riots that followed his molesters' acquittal. (Even now many whites still don't get it, as the response to the April 1996 beatings of illegal Mexican immigrants by deputies from the Riverside County Sheriff's office in South El Monte, California, proves.) Once O.J. lost his standing as a surrogate white, once he reverted back to a barbaric blackness, all bets were off. All rules were broken. Simpson began to see, perhaps for the first time, that he was worse than "just another nigger." He was a spurned black member of the white elite, an honorary white who had fallen from grace.

Simpson's celebrity, honorary whiteness, and wealth made him largely immune to the treatment shown the run-of-the-mill black male suspect. He was partly exempted by analogy: just the notion that a person *like* Simpson could murder his wife was hard for many of us to believe. The glow of false familiarity that lit his affable screen image helped too. (If one doubts the transfer between screen roles and real life, ask soap stars, who are constantly taken for their television characters, sometimes with disastrous results.) For a long stretch, Simpson made nice on television, both as a sports commentator and in typecast roles in a string of forgettable films that occasionally surface on late-night rotation. Simpson had only recently managed to find a role whose career benefit exceeded his paycheck: the hilariously unlucky Lt. Nordberg in the three *Naked Gun* films highlighted Simpson's comedic talent.

The sum of Simpson's celebrated parts—plus an unnameably perverse addiction to vicarious disintegration—moved his mostly white fans to cheer "the Juice" as he and pal A.C. Cowlings halfheartedly fled the law up I-5 and, later, the I-405 freeway in Cowlings's infamous white Bronco. (Always wanting to be like Simpson but never quite measuring up, Cowlings, this one time, ended up in the driver's seat.) Here privilege intervened. Any other black fugitive would most likely have been shot or otherwise stomped before he could call his mother, or swing by home to get a swig of orange juice. (At the time of Simpson's ungetaway cruise, LA's freeways had been the setting of the blockbuster adventure flick *Speed.* The similarities are eerie: a chase with an uncertain conclusion; a spectacle involving revenge, murder, and obsession; and the freeway itself as a metaphor for both the resolution and realization of urban trauma.)

IF SIMPSON'S CELEBRITY kept him from trauma, it attracted others to his trial to compete for public attention. Understanding that there's only so much understanding to go around—witness the spread of "compassion fatigue" and the backlash against "p.c."—abused women, blacks, feminists, and others lobbied for the trial to be viewed through the lens of their suffering. While their pain was legitimate, their perspectives were often depressingly narrow. The scamper for the spotlight ruined some. Plain old greed and self-aggrandizement spoiled others.

Still, the Simpson trial and its aftermath reveal how nefarious social forces intersect and collide, how the suffering these forces breed cuts across every imaginable line of social identity, and how the suffering of some groups outweighs the suffering of others. Domestic violence made a cameo appearance at the trial's center stage. It quickly became a bit player in the judicial drama that followed. It was shattered and swept away by a hurricane of legal strategies and tactical maneuvers. It was clear that the bodies of battered women simply don't count where they should matter most—in the public imagination, and in private spaces where women live, work, play, and, too often, where they die.

True enough, the exposure of his ugly treatment of Nicole rightly shamed Simpson. The halo Simpson wore blinded the public to the darker corners of his character. The trial deglamorized Simpson's gentle, happy-go-lucky public demeanor. At the same time, a more telling symptom of our national hypocrisy emerged. The attack on Simpson as a batterer often degenerated into scapegoating. Such a practice eases consciences. It does little, however, to erase harmful attitudes and behaviors. By demonizing Simpson, many felt they were proving the moral enlightenment of a culture that refuses to tolerate such behavior. Such self-congratulation is groundless. The demonization of Simpson amounted to little more than moral posturing. We permit, sometimes condone, the abuse and killing of women every day. We need look no further than countless courtrooms and morgues for proof. Scapegoating allows us to avoid changing the beliefs and behavior that give domestic violence secret vitality.

If we were to really change our cultural habits, calling Simpson's behavior barbaric would ring true. It would be the extension of, not the exception to, our everyday practice. In our present climate, labeling Simpson's behavior barbaric revives, however remotely, ugly stereotypes of black men as beasts. The less sophisticated version of that stereotype has long been demolished. It is reborn, however, in images of young black males as social pariahs and older black males as rootless, ruthless ne'er-do-wells. Plus, the labeling invokes the ancient taboo against interracial love, whispering to all potential Nicoles: "See, that's what happens when you mess around with a black man."

Let's face it. Beating women is a manly sport in America. It is not a widely reviled practice, at least not before the Simpson trial. (It is helpful to remind ourselves that for years many white stars in every major American sport have beat their wives, too. But without a history of stereotypes to support white male beastliness, the wife-beating issue failed to catch on among the cause célèbre set.) Simpson's treatment of Nicole—manhandling, stalking, surveilling, beating, and tyrannizing her—was vicious. It was the extreme but logical outgrowth of deeply entrenched beliefs about the worth of women's bodies in our culture. Sadly, such beliefs persist in the face of feminist activism.

Part of our problem is that we think we can have it both ways. We think we can detest feminists while lauding the "good" women, those who wouldn't call themselves feminists to save their lives. And often don't. But most men are ignorant of flesh and blood feminism and the lives of the women who fill its ranks. Feminism is what women do when they realize they must struggle to protect the rights and privileges most men take for granted.

Still, Gloria Steinem's appearance on the *Charlie Rose* show immediately after the verdicts—where she recounted taking solace in an apology offered to her, and, presumably, all whites, by an elderly black man who assured her that "not all of us feel this way"—was disappointing. It showed a lack of appreciation for the trial's complexity from a feminist who has heroically struggled for human rights. Steinem's lapse was topped, however, by the pit bull meanness of NOW's Los Angeles head, Tammy Bruce. She was later removed from office because of her relentlessly racist attacks on Simpson.

Steinem's and Bruce's behavior underlines why it is difficult for even battered black women to imagine themselves as feminists. They played the dangerous game of ranking suffering without regard to context. They made their pain, and the greater pain of abused women, the almost exclusive focus of their fiery outrage. Domestic abuse *is* a legitimate and largely neglected plague. But what Steinem and Bruce overlooked was how race gives white women's pain, and the bodies on which that pain is inflicted, more visibility than the suffering bodies of black women. There are thousands of black women who have gone to their graves at the hands of hateful men. Some of their deaths were more heinous than Nicole's. (True, they didn't have the dubious advantage of having a famous man charged with their murder.) But these women remain invisible. Even to folk like Steinem and Bruce, who are bravely committed to keeping the memory of abused women alive.

No doubt some of this resentment of unspoken white privilege—of ranking black bodies lower on the totem pole of distress—slid onto the tongues of black women who claimed the Simpson case was not about domestic violence. Technically, that's true. But neither was it, technically, about race. The important ways this case was about race are the same ways it was about domestic violence. And about the benefits and liabilities of class, wealth, fame, and gender. The disavowal of domestic abuse as an issue in the Simpson case by black women reinforces the tragic refusal of many blacks to face the crushing convergence of issues that shape black life. Their disavowal was not simply a way these women remained loyal to the script they've been handed— race first, race finally, race foremost. It was a telling example of how that script writes out their lives as well. Often in their own handwriting. The dispute between Clarence Thomas and Anita Hill showcased the futility of thinking about our problems in strictly racial terms.

There is damning evidence, too, that Nicole contributed to the brutality that broke her. And in all likelihood, killed her. I'm not arguing that Nicole should have simply left, got out at the first whiff of trouble. The destructive dance of complicity and shame, of cooperation and resistance, of instigation and retaliation, is too complex to blame victims for the brutal behavior of their abusers. And the psychology of identifying with one's abuser is too well established to mock the difficulty of leaving. But Nicole was also obsessed with O.J. Her huge appetites for cash, cocaine, and convenience tied her to a destructive lifestyle that rivaled her relationship to Simpson.

Equally tragic, Nicole's suffering was partially aided by her family's silence and inaction. Time and again Simpson hurled Nicole's body across the room. He crashed her face with his fists, leaving telltale signs almost as large as his anger. Her family surely knew or suspected that there was big trouble between Nicole and O.J. The Browns' not knowing is just as plausible as Simpson not having murdered Ron and Nicole. After Nicole's death, her sister, Denise, insisted that Nicole wasn't a battered woman. That's an excusable lie if we admit that silence, secrecy, and shame choke domestic abuse victims and their families.

Nicole's martyrdom can certainly aid other victims of domestic abuse. Her martyrdom might also help restore her family to wholeness. The Browns' helplessness and willed ignorance about Nicole's abuse—their neglect of her living body, bought in part by O.J.'s generous patronage—helped to make her a symbol of domestic violence. Her bloodied body obviously gave the Browns the energy they needed to speak up, to act. Martyrdom lifts a person's life beyond her body. Her suffering supports those who draw strength from her life's purpose—even if that purpose is only fully realized after death. The Browns must now join with others who identify, beyond blood ties or biology, with the fight against domestic violence to which Nicole's life and martyred body have become connected. Without the Browns' acknowledgment of complicity in Nicole's suffering, her martyred body becomes an empty tablet on which her family's guilt is written.

As serious as the Browns' failure was, Simpson's was by far the greater sin. His beating of Nicole marked a vile sexual obsession. Simpson apparently believed he owned

Nicole. She was a trophy. She was a commodity O.J. bought with his considerable earnings. Such logic might suggest that Nicole was interchangeable with most of the other women to whom Simpson was attracted. Like her, they had blonde hair and big breasts.

But sexual obsession is not offset by potential—by what one might have or get in the future to replace what one lost or can't have. This makes it difficult to defend Simpson by saying that he didn't have to kill Nicole because he could have had any woman he wanted. Sexual obsession can never be satisfied. The obsessor fixes on the object of desire as a way of realizing his own desire. Hence, sexual obsession is a disguised form of narcissism. It ultimately refers back to itself. Such self-reference contains the seed of the obsessor's dissatisfaction. By projecting his desire onto an erotic interest, the obsessor surrenders the means of achieving fulfillment to a force outside himself. Hence, the obsessor employs various forms of control, including seduction and violence, to bring the erotic interest in line with his wishes.

The obsessor ultimately requires the collapse of the erotic interest into himself. This feat is rarely possible, and certainly not desirable, at least not from the erotic interest's point of view. It means that the erotic interest will have to surrender her self and identity completely to the obsessor. In the obsessor's eye, to be rejected by the erotic interest is to be rejected by himself. This is a narcissist's nightmare. Such rejection is perceived as a form of self-mutilation. Or, more painfully, it is a form of self-denial. Nicole's final rejection of the sickness of her own, and O.J.'s, obsession a month before she died was the doorway to her freedom and her martyrdom. If the same act of independence led to her liberty and her death, it suggests something of the lethal obsession that millions of women live with and die from.

A SIMILARLY LETHAL OBSESSION—compounded by an even more sinister and convoluted history—shapes the course of race in this country. The responses to the verdicts were misrepresented in the media as an avalanche of emotion determined exclusively by color. Such simple scribing must never be trusted. Nevertheless, the responses showed just how sick and separate race makes us. O.J.—the figure, the trial, the spectacle, the aftermath—was a racequake. It crumbled racial platitudes. It revealed the fault lines of bias, bigotry, and blindness that trace beneath our social existence. The trial has at least forced us to talk about race. Even if we speak defensively and with giant chips on our shoulders. Race remains our nation's malevolent obsession. Race is the source of our harmony or disfavor with one another. Black and white responses to O.J. prove how different historical experiences determine what we see and color what we believe about race.

For instance, even as many blacks defended O.J., they knew he had never been one of black America's favorite sons. He didn't remember his roots when his fame and fortune carried him long beyond their influence. (Or, as a black woman wrote to me, "O.J. didn't know he had roots until they started digging.") On the surface, the black defense of Simpson can be positively interpreted. It can be viewed as the refusal of blacks to play the race authenticity game, which, in this instance, amounts to the belief that only "real" blacks deserve support when racial difficulties arise. But black responses to O.J. can also be read less charitably. They can be seen as the automatic embrace of a fallen figure simply because he is black. If you buy this line of reasoning, Simpson has a double advantage. He is eligible for insurance against the liability of racism, and he is fully covered for all claims made against him by whites, including a charge of murder. But all of these readings are too narrow. Black responses to Simpson must be viewed in light of the role race and racism have played in our nation's history. Race has been the most cruelly dominant force in the lives of black Americans. Racism exists in its own poisoned and protected world of misinformation and ignorance. Its fires of destruction are stoked by stereotype and crude mythology.

That history may help explain black support for figures like O.J. and Clarence Thomas, who have denied the lingering impact of race. Many black folk know that, in the long run, such figures remain trapped by race. Still, it is unprincipled for blacks like Thomas and Simpson to appeal to race in their defense when they opposed such appeals by other blacks in trouble. Many blacks support such figures because they think they discern, even in their exploitative behavior, a desperation, a possible seed of recognition, a begrudging concession even, that race does make a difference.

The ugly irony is that such figures get into a position to do even more harm to blacks because of the black help they receive. (Look at Thomas's judicial opinions against affirmative action and historically black colleges and universities.) For many whites, the example of race exploiters symbolizes how black Americans use race in bad faith. The problem is many whites see this only when their interests are being undermined. Simpson's offense—allowing race to be used on his behalf—is as obvious to many whites as Thomas's injury to blacks is obscured. By contrast, Thomas looks just fine to many whites. His beliefs and judicial opinions protect conservative white interests. But Thomas's cry of "high-tech lynching" when he was seeking confirmation to the Supreme Court choked off critical discussion of his desperate dishonesty. Thomas's comment was a callous, calculated attempt to win Senate votes and public sympathy by using race in a fashion he had claimed was unjust. Thomas's dishonest behavior—gaining privilege because of his blackness only to unfairly deny the same privilege to other blacks—highlights the absurdity of race for black Americans.

A small sense of the absurdity of race came crashing down on many whites when the not guilty verdicts were delivered. A surreal world prevailed. Clocks melted. Time bent. Cows flew over the moon. The chronology of race was forever split: Before Simpson and After Simpson. October 3, 1995, became a marker of tragedy. For many whites, it is a day that will live in the same sort of infamy that Roosevelt predicted for the day Pearl Harbor was bombed. It is hard to adequately describe the bewilderment many blacks felt at white rage over the verdicts. As difficult, perhaps, as it is for whites to understand how so many blacks could be deliriously gleeful at Simpson's acquittal. For perhaps the first time, the wide gulf between legality and morality became real to many whites. At least real in a way that most blacks could see whites cared about. That gulf is one blacks have bitterly protested for years, with only moderate support from most whites. The day of the verdicts, many white people were forced to think of themselves as a group—one denied special privilege rather than guaranteed it—for the first time. As a group, these whites tasted the dread, common to blacks, that follows the absolute rejection of the faith one has placed in a judicial ruling's power to bring justice. The fact that the decision officially took four hours only heaped insult on the injured souls of white folk.

In reality, however, that decision was much longer in the making. *That jury decision was set in motion the first time an American citizen, acting on behalf of the state and supported by public sentiment, made a legal judgment about a human being where an interpretation of the facts was colored by a consideration of race.* The O.J. verdicts are an outgrowth of the system started in that moment. They are, too, a painful exposure of, and a stinging rebuke to, the unjust operation of the judicial system for blacks throughout the history of our nation.

One might conclude from what I've just said that I believe the jury's decision was a rightful thumb in the justice system's eye. That it was sweet black revenge for white wrongdoing. I don't. Nor do I believe that that's the best way to read the jury's verdict. The confusion surrounding the verdicts, indeed the entire trial, reflects the confusion about the meanings of race in our culture. As far as I can see, race is being used in at least three different ways to explain the trial, especially the meaning of the verdicts. But since we haven't taken the time to figure them out, we end up collapsing them into one another in ways that are confusing and harmful. That confusion exaggerates the differences between blacks and whites. It also masks differences within black and white communities, especially where class privilege and gender are concerned.

The three uses of race I have in mind are race as *context,* race as *subtext,* and race as *pretext.* Race as context helps us to understand the *facts* of race and racism in our society. Race as a subtext helps us to understand the *forms* of race and racism in our culture. And race as a pretext helps us to understand the *function* of race and racism in America. Of course, these categories are not absolute. They are impure and flexible. They often bleed into one another. But if we're aware such distinctions exist, we have a better chance of reducing the anxiety around a highly charged subject. I'm using these categories as a tool to analyze race and as a way to describe how race and racism have affected American life. I'll briefly explore these uses of race before explaining how they might help us sort through the racial mess that the verdicts revealed.

Race as context shows how arguments have been used to clarify the role race and racism have played in our nation's history. To view race as a context leads to *racial clarification*. With racial clarification, we get down, as nearly as we can, to the facts of race. When did the idea of race emerge? Why did America choose to make distinctions among people based on race? What happened during slavery? What was Reconstruction really about? What were Abraham Lincoln's motives in freeing the slaves? How did the civil rights movement get started? What was the role of black women in the black freedom struggle of the '60s? How was black sexuality viewed during the early part of this century? How many black men were lynched before 1950? When did affirmative action start? And so on. By having these facts in hand, we're more likely to weave them into an accurate account of how race has shaped our culture. Such an account helps us tell the complex, compelling story of how race influenced ideas like democracy, justice, freedom, individuality, and equality. It also helps us to understand how racism began and spread. The most valuable use of racial clarification may be the vibrant historical framework it gives our discussions about race. It is stunning how much ignorance about what really happened in our racial past poisons present debates about race. Of course, we don't benefit from a Joe Friday "just the facts, ma'am" perspective of the past. There will be disputes about the facts and what they mean. But we certainly need to work as hard as possible to figure out what happened as we interpret the history of race.

Race as subtext highlights how arguments have been used to mystify, or deliberately obscure, the role of race and racism in our culture. To view race as a subtext aids our understanding of *racial mystification*. With this view of race, we can describe the different forms that racism takes, the disguises it wears, the tricky, subtle shapes it assumes. Race and racism are not static forces. They mutate, grow, transform, and are redefined in complex ways. Understanding racial mystification helps us grasp the hidden premises, buried perceptions, and cloaked meanings of race as they show up throughout our culture. (I realize that race and racism are not living organisms. But they have, besides an impersonal, institutional form, a quality of fretful aliveness, an active agency, that I seek to capture.)

For instance, terms like "enlightened" and "subtle" racism have been used to describe one transformation of racism: the shift from overt racism to covert forms that thrive on codes, signals, and symbols. And racial mystification was certainly at play when Charles Stuart in Boston and Susan Smith in South Carolina deflected attention from murders they had committed—Stuart of his wife, Smith of her two sons—by claiming a black man was at fault. What made their stories believable was not the fact, but the perception, of black crime. Statistically speaking, blacks overwhelmingly murder blacks, just as whites overwhelmingly murder whites. Since black males have become racially coded symbols for pathological, criminal behavior, the Stuart and Smith stories found millions of white believers. Such beliefs about black males are subtle updates of an ancient belief about black men as beasts and sexual predators. Race understood as a subtext allows us to get a handle on the changing forms of racist belief and behavior in our culture.

Finally, race as pretext shows how arguments have been used to justify racial beliefs and to defend racial interests. If the context of race is tied to history and the subtext to culture, then the pretext of race is linked, broadly speaking, to science. Race viewed as a pretext increases our understanding of *racial justification.* The stress in racial justification is on how race functions to give legitimacy to racial ideas. The proponents of racial justification drape their arguments about race in the finest garbs of science: objectivity and neutrality. After all, they are dealing in the realm of the empirical, those things that can be proved true or false by experiment and observation. Their work is often developed in the name of the sciences, natural or social. In some cases, racial justification simply seeks to supply a reasoned argument for racial preconceptions. Such arguments form a pretext to justify deeply rooted racial passions, and often give a scientific glow to racist beliefs.

For instance, Charles Murray and Richard Herrnstein's *The Bell Curve* claimed to be a work of science, a work of cool, dispassionate reason. Murray and Herrnstein simply translated racist beliefs into empirical arguments about the limits of black intelligence. Their book has been widely debunked as pseudoscience. But the enormous interest that greeted it suggests the intellectual appeal of the claims they make. The case of black psychiatrist Frances Cress Welsing is instructive as well. In her book, *The Isis Papers,* she argues for the Cress Theory of color-confrontation and racism. She links the development of white supremacist ideology to white fear of genetic annihilation. It is a biologically based argument, linked to the superiority of black skin because of its ability to produce melanin, to explain the rise of white supremacy. Welsing's theory is certainly an example of contorted reasoning used to justify racial beliefs. Viewing race as a pretext helps us to identify scientific, empirical work that attempts to justify racist beliefs.

These three uses of race and racism might help us figure out key elements of the trial. Take the bitter dispute over the "mountain of evidence." For most whites and some blacks, there was more than enough evidence to convict Simpson. Simpson had brutally battered Nicole. The blood of the victims was in his Bronco. Simpson's blood was at the crime scene. A bloody glove was found at the crime scene, its match on Simpson's estate. And above all, there were highly sophisticated DNA tests that seemed to prove Simpson's guilt beyond a reasonable doubt. But for most blacks and some whites, there was substantial doubt about the validity of the evidence, for several reasons. The reckless manner in which the evidence was collected and tested. Defense experts who testified that the evidence was questionable, inconclusive, or plain contrary to the prosecution's interpretation. And above all, the star prosecution witness, police detective Mark Fuhrman, a major collector of evidence against Simpson, who turned out to be a bigot of the worst sort.

Most whites and blacks conceded that Fuhrman's bigotry was awful. Both whites and blacks admitted that the police work was sloppy. But for most whites and a few blacks, these factors didn't matter enough to keep them from believing in Simpson's guilt. Most blacks and some whites believed that Fuhrman's mean-spirited bragging about harming, possibly killing, blacks in the past—plus the fact that he collected crucial evidence—was reason enough to doubt Simpson's guilt.

What are we to make of how black folk viewed the evidence?

Right away, race as pretext, or racial justification, makes it clear that evidence never speaks for itself. Evidence never exists in a vacuum. It is used for particular purposes.

In the Simpson case, as in any case where race is a source of contention, how we see evidence is shaped by ideological and racial interests. Evidence must be viewed through a lens of interpretation. Such a lens is surely colored by the history of race. Race as context, or racial clarification, helps us understand the facts of race that might influence how blacks view the evidence in the Simpson case in sharply different fashion from whites. There are many. The unjust treatment thousands of blacks have received at the hands of the justice system. The manufacturing of evidence against black defendants in the past. Judicial indifference to compelling evidence of a black defendant's innocence. The unequal application of punishment to black and white defendants convicted of the same crime. And repeated instances of police brutality in black communities.

Of course, the Rodney King case had already made Los Angeles blacks, indeed blacks throughout the nation, skeptical about the uses of evidence in the judicial system. Particularly when black bodies were at stake. There was, as far as most black folk were concerned, indisputable proof—if not quite the mountain of evidence amassed in the Simpson case—that police brutality was the plague they claimed it to be. After all, nobody saw Simpson murder two people. But the world saw King getting his skull smashed over and over and over again. Millions of black folk, along with the outrage they felt at the King beating, breathed a sigh of relief. Finally, here was the case that would ring the death knell for police brutality and bring the curtain down on the terror that millions of blacks feel when they're stopped by a white cop. But it was not to be. With a barrage of shrewd legal arguments, lawyers for the cops accused of King's beating made the white jury disbelieve what they saw with their own eyes. Neither could millions of blacks believe what they saw. At the trial where King's molesters were acquitted, the roar of evidence barely whimpered. Objectivity was crushed. Reason was sullied. Racial justification abounded.

To be sure, Los Angeles didn't catch fire because of a highfalutin debate about race as a pretext for the brutal treatment of blacks. It didn't erupt over intellectual disputes about the twisted uses of reason, objectivity, and evidence in the justification of racial violence. Yet these factors surely played their part in the LA riots of 1992. The seams of black civility finally burst because black folk concluded that even when they played by the rules, they could expect nothing in return—when the evidence was clear as day, it could be explained away. Of course, race as pretext and subtext converge at King's body. King was termed "bearlike," "hulklike," and "like a wounded animal" by his molesters. In view of King's assault, these terms revealed a racially mystified description that appealed to old beliefs, as I've argued above, about black males as animals. And of course, by portraying him in such racially mystified terms, the cops were able to justify their vicious treatment of King: treatment befitting a beast.

This history must be kept at the forefront of any discussion of how black folk—including the jurors—viewed the evidence against Simpson. Black response to the evidence in the Simpson case might be viewed as an example of reasonable black suspicion of the uses—really misuses—of the Enlightenment and its towering offspring: objectivity and reason. Both have been used to justify black suffering and death around the globe. Both, or at least twisted versions of the two, have led rational white folk to treat rational black folk in irrational, inhumane ways, or to overlook evidence of such behavior in their fellow whites. Plus, many blacks are suspicious of medical technology. Think of the infamous Tuskegee Study begun in 1932, when three hundred black men were used as guinea pigs to test the long-term effects of untreated syphilis. Of course, there's no direct link between such cases and the Simpson case. But such cases leave millions of blacks suspicious of the uses of sophisticated scientific technology. Especially when it is employed to prove black inferiority or to experiment with blacks as animals. A potent mix of reasonable suspicion, conspiracy theories, and paranoia thrives in pockets of black America. In the light of real abuse and suspected offenses, it is not difficult to understand how highly educated blacks could believe, for instance, that AIDS was invented to destroy black folk. Or that evidence cooked up by sophisticated science could be manufactured, distorted, or tainted to nab an innocent black man. As remote as it might seem to whites, that possibility loomed large in the Simpson case for millions of blacks. There are a thousand Mark Fuhrmans in black history. Race as context makes that fact crystal clear.

The three uses of race I've sketched might also clear up confusion about the so-called race card. The "race card" invariably referred to Johnnie Cochran's introduction of race as a factor in Simpson's trial. It referred especially to the defense's intended blasting of Mark Fuhrman, and to Cochran's statements outside the court about the pervasive nature of race in our nation. But we should make distinctions. First, the charge that Cochran played the race card is a charge of racial justification. That is, it is a charge that he used race as a pretext to argue Simpson's lack of guilt because of Fuhrman's racist behavior. That charge against Cochran is a separate issue from the validity of his point about the pervasiveness of race, which is a question of the context of race—of whether the facts, or at least an interpretation of the facts, warrant Cochran's assertion about how pervasive race is.

During the trial, and in commentary since the trial ended, the two meanings have been blurred. Cochran's point about racial pervasiveness was taken as a justification for his use of race in Simpson's defense. In fact, I think it was an attempt at racial clarification, an attempt to clarify the huge impact of race in our culture. By discussing the pervasiveness of race, Cochran sought to do a difficult thing: to talk about white racism and the privileges and penalties it bestows. It is certainly possible to disagree with Cochran's use, or interpretation, of the facts. One can argue that Cochran used legitimate facts in a distorted way. But one cannot ignore the truth of his statements about the prevalence of race in our culture. By keeping the two meanings of race separate, we won't automatically confuse speaking about the facts of race or racism with an attempt to justify unprincipled arguments or exploitative behavior.

For many whites, racial clarification and racial justification are the same. This is especially true when talking about race goes against white beliefs about the disappearance or absence of racism. The question, of course, is whether race made a difference in Simpson's case. For Cochran and millions of blacks, the reasonable answer was yes. The reasonableness of that answer is partially determined by an undeniable fact: the bad treatment of blacks by the police. Mark Fuhrman's bigoted behavior only reinforced the belief among millions of blacks that he might have framed O.J.

If we look closely, it will become clear that the race card (racial justification) was played in the Simpson trial from the very beginning. The question of which jurors to select was racially motivated. Both the defense and the prosecution took race into account. The decision to bring Christopher Darden onto the prosecution team was driven by race. The prosecution's decision to stick with Fuhrman, even when it was apparent that he was a racist, carried racial overtones. The race card had been drawn and dealt long before Cochran even came on the scene. It should be evident that the "race card" metaphor is a limited way to understand how race operates. As an instance of racial justification, the race card metaphor leaves aside the context and the subtext of race. The race card metaphor fails to account for the complexity of race. It fails to show how racism poisons civic life and denies the worth of human beings because of their color. Race is not a card. It is a condition. It is a set of beliefs and behaviors shaped by culture, rooted in history, and fueled by passions that transcend reason.

Understanding the complexity of race can throw light on the actions of the black jurors in the Simpson case. The jurors' verdicts were widely viewed as a failure to transcend race. They were also viewed, in the words of a '70s James Brown hit, as the "big payback" to whites for all the wrong they've done. Furthermore, the jurors were accused of failing to critically weigh the evidence in the case. Racial clarification helps to identify a historical paradox of race for blacks relating to claims of this sort: when dealing with their peers, blacks are seen as fair—that is, neutral, just, and transcending race—only when they oppose perceived black interests. For many whites, the black jurors could only transcend race, and satisfy the demands of justice and good citizenship, by finding Simpson guilty of murder. Because the jury found Simpson not guilty, many whites believed their decision was an instance of racial justification, that the verdicts were a biased judgment, a pretext for racial solidarity.

But blacks routinely convict black defendants. (I should know. I saw my brother sentenced to life in prison by an all-black jury.) Neither are whites viewed as unfair when they fail to send a white defendant to jail. Whites are not viewed in such cases as expressing white solidarity. Unless, of course, the defendant is accused of a crime against a black person. Even then, whites defend their decisions as just. They often claim their decisions are made without regard to color. Whites are rarely asked to consider the role race plays in the decisions they make. This is especially the case when their decisions involve unconscious expressions of group loyalty.

Racial mystification may help to explain veiled, and not-so-veiled, references to the black jurors' intelligence. The subtext of criticisms aimed at the black jurors was drenched in race: they were uneducated, hence, intellectually inferior. It's interesting to note how dismissed white juror Francine Florio-Bunten's story casts light on racial mystification in the trial. Florio-Bunten claims she would have voted to convict Simpson. She has been celebrated, in coded terms, as a white heroine who would have saved the day by representing the "truth"—that is, "white" interests. Florio-Bunten was lauded for being the only juror who knew what "DNA" stood for at the beginning of the trial. (The subtext is that the black jurors, by contrast, were dumb.) Florio-Bunten also claims that she had decided Simpson's guilt long before the trial had ended. Yet, unlike the black jurors, who were viciously attacked for arriving at a hasty decision (after four hours of deliberation), Florio-Bunten has been exempt from harsh criticism. Florio-Bunten is even more ingratiating to whites when she claims that no amount of deliberation by her cohorts would have swayed her opinion. (Subtext: she would have resisted "black interests" and stood firm for "white interests.") The stigma black jurors wear—dumb, race loyalists, un-American—is the stigma attached to many blacks who risk white rage by reaching decisions that upset white interests and beliefs.

IN THE FINAL ANALYSIS, what race as context, race as subtext, and race as pretext cannot help us gain is certainty about the motives that lurk in the hearts of human beings. We don't know what intentions or motivations people have apart from the behavior we can observe. (That is the frustration for blacks confronting subtle forms of racism that are not manifest in overt action.) Despite every effort to explain the jury's actions, it may be that race, of whatever sort, was the motivation for their decision in the Simpson trial. No amount of knowledge or insight can protect against that possibility. Black folk already know this because they have been on the losing end of that proposition too many times before. As this case proves, it's a bitter lesson few whites are familiar with. It may be that the jurors' decision confirmed the worst fears of whites and blacks: Despite what many whites think about blacks—that they are morally inferior— or what many blacks think about themselves—that they are morally superior to whites—blacks and whites may be very much the same.

Oddly enough, that might be a basis for moving beyond the prison of race. Not by denying race, but by taking it into account. That is the lesson we learn from clarifying our understanding of race. Those whites who claim it is unfair, even absurd, for blacks to enjoy racial preferences deny that whites have always enjoyed such preferences on a much larger scale. Now that many whites seek to use the absurdity of racial preferences as a justification for axing programs like affirmative action, they fail to make use of history. True enough, they highlight the absurdity of the idea of race. But they remove it from a context—racial clarification—that explains its historical function—to justify white privilege. The bitter history of black struggle, the facts, are what make the idea that race is absurd valid and compelling.

To take that idea out of context and to turn it against blacks without regard for history is crass and dishonest.

Then, too, blacks must be honest about the manner in which we have been vulnerable to race exploiters who deny the importance of race. If racial justice is our dominant concern, then the cases of prisoners Geronimo Pratt and Mumia Abu-Jamal should have goaded us to action long before the superrich Simpson captured our attention. And our large disinterest in the trials of rappers Snoop Doggy Dogg, Tupac Shakur, and Dr. Dre reveals a huge class and generational bias in black America. In fact, millions of blacks believed the hostile portrayals of these young blacks in the media. (I'm not suggesting that each didn't deserve criticism for his actions. I'm simply referring to hostile black reaction to the category of "young, black male" or "rapper.") Millions of blacks believed in these rappers' probable guilt simply because they were rappers. Millions of blacks didn't rally around these rappers, who probably had more cash than Simpson. Many blacks wrote them off. Why? They weren't the right kind of blacks. They weren't "our" kind of role models. Yet such figures, given the wide public hostility aimed at them, are more likely to be targets of white fear and police misconduct than a rich, well-loved black sports icon like O.J. Class divisions in black life are huge and growing.

In the end, we can only have racial progress if we take the lessons of this case seriously. Despite the undeniable advances we have made, despite the enormous strides taken, we remain a deeply divided society. (Although this case framed our racial problems in black and white, we must certainly realize that there are all sorts of racial and ethnic tensions brewing that involve Asian, Native American, and Latino communities.) We cannot wish our differences away. We must work to increase our understanding of the contexts, pretexts, and subtexts of race. Then we must do something concrete about racial suffering and racial injustice. We have the negative examples of O.J. Simpson and Mark Fuhrman, the two men at the center of this trial, to spur us on past their, and our, tragic limitations and failures. Simpson, in particular, is a man without a country. The white folk who once adored him, and whose acceptance Simpson still seeks, now despise him. The blacks Simpson has never shown much interest in, and who have welcomed him, do not inspire his allegiance.

In perhaps one of the most tragic ironies this case has served up, a black man who lived his life avoiding black culture was ultimately set free because of a white bigot who hated blacks and worked at the core of urban black life. The cruel symmetry of their fates at the hands of a black culture that each, in his own way, found troubling is nearly biblical.

Interestingly, a group of black intellectuals has found fame and fortune by embracing black culture. In a world far removed from the playing field, these figures both depend on their race, and, to some extent, deny it, in order to win both compensation and adulation. The ideas of race these figures defend are, like Simpson, however, steeped in controversy.

TWO

It's Not What You Know, It's How You Show It

Black Public Intellectuals

Distracted, instead, by false or secondary issues, yielding apparently little resistance to the sound intrusion of market imperatives on the entire intellectual object, including that of African American studies, today's creative black intellectual lends herself/himself—like candy being taken from a child—to the mighty seductions of publicity and the "pinup"...Might it be useful, then, to suggest that before the black creative intellectual can "heal" her people, she must consider to what extent she must "heal" herself?

Hortense Spillers
"The Crisis of the Negro Intellectual: A Post-date," 1994

GENTLE READER, I BEGIN this chapter with a confession and a warning. First, the warning. This is not an objective examination of the contentious debates surrounding the rise of so-called black public intellectuals. (You haven't heard of us? Well, the debates are mostly "inside baseball." To tell the truth, the debates are more like inside-the-academy bickering. Okay, you've got me: they're tempests in teapots, even though the teapots are pretty prestigious. But if it's any consolation, the debates offer the same sort of mudslinging, backbiting, gossiping, and dozens-playing you're likely to find in a supermarket tabloid.) Mine is a partisan account of how black intellectuals got into the fix of being lauded and lambasted, admired and despised, in the same breath. This is simply one black public intellectual's teeth-baring, tongue-in-cheek mea culpa and apologia rolled into one.

Now the confession: I have been chosen as one of the lucky few. I have been the recipient of great praise (and sharp criticism, but more on that later) for my writing and speaking at universities and before the general public. Along with a relatively few others—including Henry Louis Gates, Cornel West, bell hooks, Robin Kelley, Patricia Williams, and Stephen Carter—I've been dubbed a public intellectual. This designation emphasizes how our work contributes to public debate, especially about race and American society. The term public intellectual is certainly not new. It's been applied to a range of scholars and intellectuals throughout Europe and America. Other terms, like political intellectual and organic intellectual, hint at the same public function for the thinker. The term public intellectual gained fresh currency in the late '80s with the publication of Russell Jacoby's book, *The Last Intellectuals.*

But never before has such a highly educated and vastly literate group of black thinkers had access to the Public Mind of America—and acclaim or derision for managing to do so. We have been hailed and harangued by publications ranging from the *New Yorker* and the *Atlantic Monthly* to the *Village Voice*. And most of us have appeared on *Oprah Winfrey, Charlie Rose, Nightline,* and a spate of other television shows, to talk about a range of subjects, and a lot about race. So I've got no complaints about the publicity my work receives. (Well, I've got a few, but they're the carps of the privileged, so I'll spare you.) I've been very fortunate indeed.

You'd think that academics everywhere, especially black ones, would be proud, that they'd see in our achievements their investments in us, and those like us, paying all sorts of dividends. Increased visibility for the profession. Heightened respect for black intellectual work. And a celebration of the unsung giants, especially the black ones, on whose shoulders we all stand. And many, many scholars and intellectuals do brim with pride and joy. But a lot don't. They simmer in resentment and prophesy trouble. Much of what makes them troubled is legitimate. Then, too, much of their resentment stems from pettiness, parochialism, and snobbishness.

In my case, as with many other black public intellectuals, there has been a strident, severe, but altogether predictable "blacklash." I've been called a "sellout." Cornel West's work has been viciously dismissed as "completely worthless." bell hooks has been assailed for being "a hustler." After my appearance on *Nightline* to talk about making the Million Man March more than a walk for testosterone or bigotry, I was accused of playing "Goebbels," the shrewd and perverted Nazi propagandist, to Farrakhan's Hitler. (Yeah, that's pretty libelous, but the guy who wrote it is named Adolf—I guess it was a case of vicarious nostalgia.) As you can tell, things have gotten nasty. What's the problem?

According to critics, there are several. First, there is the question of how the few of us who are deemed public intellectuals got anointed. Second, our work suffers from an intellectual thinness that could be remedied if only we weren't busy pontificating, prophesying, or playing pundit on television or radio. Third, the prestige, fame, and fortune bestowed on us are corrupting, making us sellouts. Fourth, we public intellectuals play an authenticity game, claiming to speak as politically rooted prophets for The Race as we peddle distorted meanings of blackness to the undiscerning white masses. Fifth, we're treated with kid gloves by colleagues and not really criticized. Finally, we all want to be HNIC (for the uninitiated, Head Negro In Charge).

Let's face it, there's some truth to some of these charges, and, depending on whom we're talking about, there's a lot of truth to many of these charges. Still, we don't have to give up on being public intellectuals. It's an honorable, even critical vocation. After all, just because counterfeit money exists, we don't have to stop spending the real thing. (Uh-oh, maybe the criticism about materialism is right; it's even seeping into my analogies!) We've just got to pay attention to fair criticisms, confess our masked and bald opportunism, admit that we're susceptible to the seductions of fame and fortune, and acknowledge that there are other equally gifted intellectuals who could do what we do, maybe even better. We've also got to face head-on the vicious personal attacks that get palmed off as brave commentary. And we've got to call a spade a spade: there's a lot of jealousy out here.

The irony of all this infighting and name-calling is that just as black intellectuals begin to receive our due—that is, a few of us, which, as you *can't* tell by the fury of the complaints, is more than received it in the past, the rule being the less there is to go around the more you fight over who gets it—we begin to knock each other off. Or others do the job for us. Hateful assaults from black and white writers often reveal their ignorance, or their distorted views, of how we got where we are. There's a difference between sharp criticism and the animus of ad hominem and ad feminem roasting. Sure, when you're the object of even the healthy kind of criticism, it can sting for days. And sometimes a literate intellectual licking leaves you feeling like you've been mugged by a metaphor. But you gird your loins to write again.

Why are so many critics hot and blathered?

The anointing of a few voices to represent The Race is an old, abiding problem. For much of our history, blacks have had to rely on spokespersons to express our views and air our grievances to a white majority that controlled access to everything from education to employment. For the most part, powerful whites only wanted to see and hear a few blacks at a time, forcing us to choose a leader—when we could. Often a leader was selected for us by white elites. Predictably, blacks often disagreed with those selections, but since the white elites had the power and resources, their opinions counted.

Such an arrangement created tensions in black communities because it reduced blackness to its lowest common denominator. Only what could be condensed into speeches, editorials, and other public declarations survived transmission to white elites. Complexity was often sacrificed for clarity. It also made the content of what was communicated about black culture conform to the spokesperson's gifts, vision, or interests. Thus, a spokesperson had a profound impact on what goods or services the rest of his or her black constituency received. The accountability of such leaders was often low.

Complicating matters further was the fact that the choice of spokespersons didn't always turn on issues that were of greatest interest or importance to blacks. Often a spokesperson was selected because his themes, style, and ideology were acceptable to the white majority. Many black leaders were viewed skeptically by their constituencies. Booker T. Washington is a prime example of this model of leadership.

Naturally, these conditions introduced considerable tension into the relationship between those who did the speaking and those who were spoken for. Black spokespersons acquired influence because they were given legitimacy by the white majority, whose power to establish such legitimacy was far greater than that of the black minority. As a result, these spokespersons used their power in black communities to reward loyal blacks and to punish dissidents. This arrangement meant that patronage more than moral principle determined the allocation of the limited resources for which the spokesperson was a funnel. As a result, few blacks benefited from the leadership that was supposed to speak for them all.

This legacy of anointment and appointment hangs like a stone cloud over the debate about black public intellectuals. Who gets to be a black public intellectual, who chooses them, and what have they done for you lately? We can answer these questions by first posing a more basic question: Why are black public intellectuals presently enjoying such prominence?

The fact that race is being bitterly debated as *the* national issue has a lot to do with the rise of black public intellectuals. Race has always been a deep, characteristic American problem. The refusal to face race, or our courageous confrontation with its complex meanings, defines our national identity. And it goes in cycles. At some points in our nation's history—for instance, during the civil rights movement—we were forced to contend with race. At other times, such as during the erosion of racial progress in the Reaganite '80s, we believed we could just as well do without all those remedies like affirmative action, which, in any case, had been manufactured to give a leg up to undeserving blacks. Well, Edgar Allan Poe met Yogi Berra: the pendulum of race has swung back, and it's déjà vu all over again. Race is once more an inescapable force on a variety of fronts: the school yard, the job market, the justice system, politics, everywhere we look. So, living down to the crude, stereotypical version of American pragmatism, we call in the race experts to tell us what's going on.

The enhanced currency of black public intellectuals also rides the wave of popularity that sections of black life are enjoying. If there's one fact of black life in white America we can't deny, it's this: black folk go in and out of style. Most of the time our identities are exploited for white commercial ends, or ripped off to further the careers of white imitators. Blackness is today a hot commodity, but of course, it always has been: the selling of black bodies on the slave market, minstrel shows, Elvis's cloning of black gospel and blues singers all point to the fetish of black skin and skill in American popular culture. Once the barriers to black achievement were lowered, black folk ourselves got more of the fat.

Black bodies are "in" now, that is, if you don't happen to be a black man with a car, tangling with the police in Los Angeles or the white suburbs of Pittsburgh. Rodney King was the LA driver, and, well, you know what happened to him and to all of us because of what the police did and what the white jury didn't do. Jonny Gammage was the second driver, and he was stopped and subsequently choked to death by white police because he was wheeling his football star cousin Ray Seals's sports car in a neighborhood where everybody knows a black man shouldn't drive. You're alright if your black body shows up on professional basketball courts, where nearly 80 percent of the players are black. Or in the entertainment industry, where, despite the preponderance of decent parts doled out to whites, more blacks have slightly thicker pickin's and more leftovers to compete for than in the past. And hip-hop culture, to the chagrin of a whole lot of black folk, has literally darkened the face—some would say given it a black eye—of popular music.

Because black folk are leaving their mark all over American culture, there are renewed debates about what blackness means. Who better to call on than those blacks who spend their lives thinking, writing, and living black experience. (I can see it now: The film features our heroes being summoned to city hall to fight the slime and sludge of racism, backed by the refrain of the movie's theme song—"Who you gonna call? RACEBUSTERS! I ain't afraid of no racist.") As terrible as the fallout from all the fuss about black public intellectuals is—that is, as limited and limiting as the focus on a few elites is—at least some of us have a small say in what's done, or more modestly, in what's thought about black folk.

That's a significant improvement over the times when white critics pontificated about blackness without knowing, or in some cases, caring much about the subject. Even when white critics were righteous, when they were honest and critically sympathetic and did their homework, they were the only ones allowed to speak about black culture to the masses. If black folk weren't allowed in the front of the bus, at the top of white classes, or in the major leagues—about the only place they were invited to be first was, when they could enlist, at the war's front line—they certainly weren't going to be delivering astute analyses of their kith and kin to millions on television, radio, or in newspapers.

As usual, however, a blessing brings burdens. Some white critics have pointed out—some lamenting, others fuming—what a terrible thing it is for blacks to talk only about race, and that for them to make race their sole subject is, in the long run, harmful to the image of black intellectuals as perpetual one-noters. True enough. But a little clarification is in order. Black thinkers fought hard for Americans to take race seriously, that is, as an object of legitimate, critical examination. Early white thinkers, people like David Hume and Thomas Jefferson, resisted the process, outside of scandalously biased interpretations of black culture that masqueraded as scientific treatises on the inferiority of black culture. It was not until well into this century that white scholars began to study race for greater intellectual purposes than the proof of white superiority and the redemption, however crudely managed, of black savages. So black intellectuals paid the cost to be the boss in a realm of experience in which their thinking on the subject was usually overlooked, discounted, or berated.

Also, criticisms of the racial monomania of black intellectuals sometimes miss how black thinkers have been discouraged from making comment in public about issues other than race. The year he died, Malcolm X noted how even when whites "credit a Negro with some intelligence," they still feel the black thinker is only qualified to speak about race. "Just notice how rarely you will hear whites asking any Negroes what they think about the problem of world health or the space race to land men on the moon," Malcolm remarked in 1965.

That's still true today. Black intellectuals are rarely asked about the collapse of communism, the crisis of capitalism, whether cigarettes should be banned in public spaces, the successes and failures of feminism, the Palestinian-Israeli conflict, the state of modern Islam, the transcendentalist vision of Emerson, Walt Whitman's beliefs about erotic friendship, the impact of Heisenberg's uncertainty principle on the debate about postmodernism, Foucault's notion of power, Walt Disney's role in pop culture, fin-de-siècle apocalyptic thinking, Russian formalism, Murray Perahia's Beethoven concertos, and a world of things besides. We're rarely even asked about the unusual things black folk do, like scuba diving, writing histories of German warplanes, studying ancient Chinese cultures, and so on.

So before critics ascend their high horses too quickly, they should dig their intellectual spurs into the beast of history and hold on for the long, rough ride. Black intellectuals turned a deficit into a credit. They were limited to writing, or speaking in public, about race. As a result, the subject is now viewed the way black intellectuals have long viewed it, as the central problem of American society, through the eyes of thinkers who have witnessed the bitter triumphs of racism while working feverishly for its defeat. Just because the rest of the world caught on much later—and to be fair, many whites have fought side by side with blacks from the very beginning—is no reason to punish those, or at least their descendants, who got the point in the first place.

It is important to remember that contemporary black public intellectuals do have forebears. That would certainly temper whatever pride or self-satisfaction some black public intellectuals might feel about their present fortunes. They didn't fall out of the sky, fully formed and prepared to contest the demons of race. Black intellectuals learned at the knees of, and sometimes, unfortunately, at the expense of, black thinkers who blazed the paths we now travel. Too often, these pioneers were cut off from the public they coveted, their writings deprived of the close and critical readings they so richly deserved.

E. Franklin Frazier, renowned sociologist and the first black president of the American Sociological Association, was restricted within the broader, whiter world of academia in which he was trained and over which he had at least nominal influence. And W.E.B. Du Bois, the universally recognized Thomas Jefferson of black letters, the founder of black intellectual invention in the twentieth century, and the first black to earn a Ph.D. from Harvard, was prevented from sharing his genius with the institution that shaped him. As the strange career of race has evolved, the anatomy of opportunity for blacks has changed as well. The post-civil rights generation of black intellectuals has begun to get some of the benefits that even towering intellectual giants were routinely denied. For the most part, the present cadre of celebrated black intellectuals is the first generation to gain entry as students into elite white colleges and universities, later to return and find their voices and vocations within those same halls of ivy as professors.

But even that progress contains a drawback. Much of the attention has been given to those black intellectuals who have managed to find—and hog—the public spotlight. Less attention has been paid to their cohort in universities for whom the classroom and careful scholarship are enough. (Or to community college teachers whose commitment to educating black folk is undervalued.) Such scholars—shall we call them, for want of a better term, black private intellectuals?—have been, by virtue of the dramatic emphasis placed on the public intellectuals, done a grave disservice.

The cruel irony is that just as black scholars have attained legitimate standing in the academy, getting it the old-fashioned way, by earning tenure, writing scholarly monographs, and publishing learned articles, they now have to compete for attention with so-called black public intellectual superstars. Such figures are the pampered, high-profile elite who command large speaking fees; get their books reviewed in all the right, bright-light, high-gloss magazines and newspapers; appear on television to chat about their latest work; and occasionally represent the hard-working, low-wage-earning, undereducated black masses. (Sometimes these intellectuals secretly compete with the masses in their own minds, as they recall their latest critical rebuff or exaggerate their own suffering, seeing it as the moral equivalent of welfare, class warfare, and income inequality.)

In other words, not only do private black intellectuals have to put up with all the mess they take from a white academy that is often still insensitive and hostile, they now have to hear about the goings-on of black public intellectuals, who are the supposed proof that not only do black scholars have it good, they've got it better than most white academics. What a bind. (Of course, given the levels of hostility now being directed at black public intellectuals within the academy, the private intellectuals might use their status to their advantage: "Oh, no, not me. I'm not a public intellectual. I'm just a poor working stiff who grades papers, attends faculty meetings, serves on committees, writes articles and books, and, in what spare time I have, I volunteer for the neighborhood literacy project.")

As we grouch, sometimes with good reason, about the narrowness and limitations of the university, black public intellectuals should remember that it is the foothold we found inside the academy—before we "went public"—that became our launching pad for fame and fortune in the first place. The academy is still home, and our criticisms shouldn't feed into the hysterical rantings against the academy by the far right that leave our private intellectual colleagues, especially black ones, most vulnerable. Many conservatives believe the university is a den of politically correct educational thieves, robbing our kids of their moral futures with all sorts of strange theories.

Well, the university isn't all it's cracked down to be: an artificial environment removed from the lives of real people. Last time I checked at my university, there were actual bodies in the classroom, real people running the place, and life-and-death issues being fought over by people who will one day run businesses, defend clients, make millions, enrich lives, ruin government, and become politicians (sorry for the repetition) in the Real World. Be glad—okay, some of you should be sorry—that many of my colleagues get a crack at them first. Some esoteric theory, off-the-cuff comment, or chance encounter with someone completely opposite in viewpoint might make the difference, a quarter century after a student leaves a classroom, in her doing the right or wrong thing.

Sure, the alleged Unabomber went to Harvard and Michigan. But before that he lived in Chicago's white suburbs, and after he dropped out of the academy he haunted the mountains of Montana. And no one's going to argue that, based on their influence on his outlook, either place should be destroyed. (I simply can't resist noting, with all the unfairness and smallness of perspective my comment implies, that the alleged Unabomber's genius was quantitative; maybe if he'd had more humanities courses, he could have dropped rhetorical, not literal, bombs!)

Not only is the problem of the black private intellectual compelling, but, if we're honest, the current crop of black public intellectuals is selected in a way that's elitist and incestuous. Most of us went to Ivy League schools, few of the official designees teach outside of elite eastern schools, and none teach at historically black colleges and universities. I'm not aiming here at some sort of compensatory principle for the sake of including all segments of the black intellectual community. I'm simply pointing out that if the criterion for being a public intellectual is the ability to speak and write clearly and substantively about important public issues for broad audiences, then many, many more black scholars fit the bill. Black scholars like William Strickland, Jerry Ward, Gloria Wade-Gayles, Beverly Guy-Sheftall, Ethelbert Miller, and a host of others certainly qualify. And God knows that black nationalist and Afrocentric scholars like Ron Karenga, Molefi Asante, Asa Hilliard, Ivan Van Sertima, Na'im Akbar, and LaFrances Rogers Rose were doing public intellectual work, especially among despised, invisible black communities, way before the term took hold.

Certainly that's part of the catch. Contemporary black public intellectuals are valued because we speak—by no means exclusively, and, in some cases, not even primarily, but nonetheless in important ways—to a *white* public. We are involved, however much we might not like it, with the translation, interpretation, explanation, and demystification of black culture to white masses. The temptations are readily apparent. That we become the judges of authentic blackness. That we become viewed as the most visible, and hence, the most important and informed interpreters of black culture. That we hoodwink naive white folk with a racial abracadabra whose plausibility depends upon their ignorance. That we misrepresent the cantankerous ideological and cultural differences within black life. That we come to think white folk are the only folk that count and, in trying to please them, we end up selling out black interests.

One black writer harshly reproved black public intellectuals for explaining the heart of black darkness to white folk, saying that we based our claims on being Real Blacks as we make big cash telling white folk about the ins and outs of black culture. According to him, we were conniving, careerist sellouts. He made that charge, of course, in the well-known black weekly, the *Village Voice,* gaining a reputation for tough talk, and a column in that publication to boot. Who says trashing black intellectuals for selling out to whites doesn't pay off handsomely, giving the critic, in this case a black intellectual, more visibility, a larger public voice, and more legitimacy in the white world?

Let's get real. Black folk read the papers, watch television, and consume books like everybody else. In fact, much has been made of the strong and still increasing numbers of black book buyers. Black public intellectuals are reaching broader white *and* black audiences through their work. Only by underestimating the intelligence of those audiences can we conclude that black public intellectuals will get away with too much rhetorical or intellectual legerdemain. Besides, most of the black public intellectuals I know make regular appearances among black folk to hash out important ideas about race, democracy, and this nation's destiny. In fact, many of the black folk who show up to see and argue with these figures read their books, saw them on television, read their articles in newspapers, or heard them on the radio.

Mass media have changed the stakes for the black intelligentsia. Even when Du Bois, Frazier, Zora Neale Hurston, or Langston Hughes held forth in black communities, they didn't have anything like the range of audience or publicity today's black scholars enjoy. Television, radio, newspapers, and now the Internet have changed all that. Now that black intellectuals regularly appear on the *Today* show and National Public Radio, and in the pages of the *New York Times,* the *New Yorker,* the *Los Angeles Times,* and the like, they have more visibility and name recognition than many of their predecessors.

It's easy to see why many critics think that's a bad thing. First, such critics play an authenticity game themselves, that follows this line of reasoning: Real scholars read, write, study, and reflect at home or in the university. The virtue of their work often rests in its ability to critically and carefully examine a subject with as much rigor and intellectual responsibility as they can muster. While their findings may apply directly to public life, their work will be read—and critics don't often say this—mainly by other academics and graduate students. Sounds good to me. I've written stuff like that, with no apologies, because as a black person, then a black scholar, I've learned that we really have little choice but to master many languages, arcane theoretical ones and eloquently lucid ones as well.

But that's not the only valid, compelling model of scholarship available. To put it simply, we need both: serious, critical reflection away from the lights, cameras, and action of the public realm; and gritty, graceful, engaged intellectual work that takes on the issues of the day with force and fire. Some of us can do both, while many of us can only master one. There's no shame either way. The elitist, snobbish attempt to say only traditional scholarly work counts is self-serving. It's also an intellectually bigoted view of the life of the mind. On the other hand, the attempt to equate fame or notoriety with intellectual achievement is vicious and small-minded.

At some point, the claim that the work of black public intellectuals is simply not rigorous enough, that its intellectual predicates are too thin, can be legitimately made about all public intellectuals. I know it's true of some of my work. (Please, don't ask what work I'm referring to; I might have to tell you which paragraph of an essay I wrote when I was twelve that I have in mind.) We all slip. And our critics should be there to catch us. But the genre of public intellectual work is not itself indictable on that charge, as some critics want us to believe. True enough, we can't equate an op-ed piece on the unfairness of sending blacks to jail in disproportionate numbers with a dense description of the ways criminality has functioned to stigmatize black folk in America. The latter will, if well done, do much to reorient thinking among scholars who influence the perception of these matters in academic circles, and, by extension, beyond the academy. The former could pull the coat of some policy wonk or congressional flunky who might pass it on to her boss. Both sorts of work are worthwhile.

What's doubly intriguing about the debate over lack of rigor, especially among black intellectuals, is that, like the mourners at a funeral, those crying the loudest are the most guilty. I've seen, heard, and participated in too many discussions with self-styled rigorous black intellectuals (shall we call them the rigorighteous?) who took special pride in the complexity, nuance, and density of their thinking—while despising the lack of same in the work of other black intellectuals—who were then denied tenure by their white colleagues for lack of substantive work, and laughed at behind their backs by those they seek to please with their displays of rigorous wizardry. There's a useful distinction to be made between rigor, which can be expressed in elegant prose or in complex theory, and wanton inaccessibility, which masquerades as cutting-edge intellectual craft when it's little more than jargon-bloated, obfuscated intellectual nonsense.

Make no mistake. This is not a mini-broadside against post-modernism, poststructuralism, or any of the influential pillars, like Derrida and Foucault, of those posts. At its best, theory should help us unmask the barbarous practices associated with some traditions of eloquent expression. But like a good sermon or a well-tailored suit, theory shouldn't show its seams.

Black scholars—though this is true for other scholars as well, just not with the same implications about presence or lack of intelligence—are often put in a "damned if you do, damned if you don't" bind. On the one hand, we were told for years that our work was worthless, that it lacked the rigor and language by which serious scholarly work is known. We were subtly but insistently implored to employ the jargon of our disciplines, thereby showing our mastery of that plot of intellectual ground we were taught to plow. Then we were told that if our scholarly writings were too jargon-filled they were obtuse and meaningless. We were told that if we couldn't write in ways that made sense to a broad public our work was of no use. This is good to remember now that critics are taking black public intellectuals to task for our work. Back when scholars like Oliver Cox and W.E.B. Du Bois were doing just what it is alleged we often don't do—careful, serious, deeply thoughtful work—they were ignored or dismissed. Du Bois's monumental study, *Black Reconstruction,* sold only 376 copies in its first year of publication in 1935. The book wasn't even reviewed by the *American Historical Review,* the leading journal in the historical profession. That's a sober reminder of how black intellectuals shouldn't be too quick to surrender whatever visibility we've managed to secure in deference to a notion of scholarly propriety. We see where that got us.

It's also evident that the lure of the lights can corrupt black intellectuals by making us believe our own press. Or by making us addicted to praise and disdainful of serious criticism, which, by the way, every public intellectual lauds as a virtue, except when it's directed his or her way. Nobody hates criticism like a critic. Still, many black public intellectuals have been victims of drive-by, gangster-style criticism. In this sort of attack, one can virtually hear the machinery of jealousy working overtime to crush another black intellectual's work, to knock her reputation down a few notches to build up the critic's own. No one but the critic benefits from such hateful exercises.

Equally worrisome, too many black public intellectuals hog the ball and refuse to pass it to others on their team. Many times I've been invited on a television program, a prestigious panel, or a national radio program because a white critic or intellectual recommended me. Later I often discover that another prominent black public intellectual, when consulted, had conveniently forgotten to mention my name or that of other qualified black intellectuals. Ugly indeed.

I guess this is a way of saying that, yes, a lot of black public intellectuals, despite what we say—maybe because we say we don't—really do want to be HNIC, which, in light of the fierce and corrupting competition over the sweepstakes of visibility, also means Hottest Negro In the Country. If that's the case, it's a disgusting waste of a grand opportunity for a group of black intellectuals to make a significant impact on our nation's debates about race and blackness. By doing that well, we might open up space for black thinkers to range freely over the entire field of American interests. Black public intellectuals have a great responsibility: to think clearly, to articulate eloquently, to criticize sharply, to behave humanely, and to raise America's and black folks' vision of what we might achieve if we do away with the self-destructive habit of racism and the vicious forces of black self-defeat taking us down from within.

BLACK PUBLIC INTELLECTUALS ARE leaders of a particular kind. We stir up trouble in broad daylight so that the pieties by which we live and the principles for which we die, both as a people and a nation, are subject to critical conversation. Black public intellectuals are certainly not leaders in the sense as, say, Jesse Jackson or Louis Farrakhan, with an identifiable base in black communities from which we launch criticism or commentary that often, though not always, reflects our constituencies' beliefs. Not that black public intellectuals don't have what might be considered constituencies. There are many publics, and black public intellectuals move in and out of many of them, including the university. Sure the university is not, nor should it be, a civil rights organization, although some crotchety conservatives and miffed liberals would argue that multiculturalism, identity politics, and "p.c." have made the differences between the two rather small. But the university is a public sphere, with a lot of rich people's and poor people's kids attending. And given the attention we've got, black public intellectuals have to try to help make the world smarter, safer, and saner for those, and all of America's, youth. We don't speak for The Race. We speak as representatives of the ideological strands of blackness, and for those kinships we possess outside of black communities, that we think are most healthy.

But we ain't messiahs. Nor should we have messiah complexes. We can't afford to take our world's problems lightly. But we certainly can't afford to take ourselves too seriously. In that spirit, Gentle Reader, I offer you as a send-off—

perhaps even a send-up—a summary of what I think about black public intellectuals and our critics. Since we're not, for the most part, eligible for Oscars, Grammys, or Emmys, consider these the Envys, given to recipients of the First Annual Awards for Black Public Intellectuals and Their Critics.

THE CHEAPER BY THE DOZENS AWARD.   This award is given to Adolf Reed and Eric Lott, two very smart, if mean-spirited, scholars who revel in ad hominem and ad feminem arguments. Reed wrote an essay about black public intellectuals in the *Village Voice,* heaping personal attacks on me and bell hooks ("little more than hustlers"), Cornel West (whom Reed in the past called "a thousand miles wide and about two inches deep"), Robin Kelley, and Skip Gates. Reed called me and West "running dogs" for Farrakhan in another *Voice* article (but we must not be too well heeled—we still didn't get a chance to speak at the Million Man March)! Reed's bitter commentary seems based more on a writer's level of success with the public than on anyone's actual ideas, since he is so damn mad at so many different thinkers!

Lott, too, has taken to personal attacks, especially in the left journal *Social Text,* where he called West a sellout, and in the journal *Transition,* where he labeled my work "middlebrow imbecilism" (just to think, most people have to meet me twice to draw that conclusion). For both writers, we black public intellectuals just aren't radical enough. But isn't that argument worn out by now? At their worst, Reed and Lott prove that the left continues to do what it seems to do best: self-destruct! The left holds firing squads in a circle, while our real "enemies"—the radical right-wingers who detest every bone in our progressive heads (I'm sorry, I mean bodies)—get off scot-free!

THE ELIJAH COMPLEX AWARD. This award is named after the Biblical figure who cried, "I, even only I, am left," proclaiming himself the only true prophet in town. It goes to the undeniably brilliant bell hooks for the numerous times she's told us, in writing, in public, or in conversation, how she's the only black intellectual to talk about class, or the only black on a panel to get the deeper dimensions of the topic of conversation, or one of the few black feminists who's a serious intellectual. Somebody tell bell that God told Elijah, "Sorry, but there are 7,000 others like you still around." Well, maybe there aren't that many black feminists and serious intellectuals who talk about class, and about race, and gender and sex, too, but there are a whole lot more than bell seems to be aware of. Please, somebody give her a list!

THE SPIKE LEE/TERRY MCMILLAN AWARD FOR SHAMELESS SELF-PROMOTION. Okay, I'm the recipient of this award, for calling newspapers, television and radio stations, magazines, and other venues to tell them why they needed to review my book, or have me on to talk about my work. I can't believe I'm telling this. After all, I wanted people to believe my name was so hot that folk just couldn't stand to run special issues of journals, assemble conferences, or do shows on the matters that I address without me. And you thought the black public intellectual's job was easy. Listen, if there are any publishers, magazine editors, or television producers reading, I'd like to tell you about my latest book...

THE GOLDA MEIR "HUMILITY IS MY STRONG SUIT" AWARD. Meir once said, "Stop being humble, you're not that great." This goes to the very talented Cornel West, who genuinely is very humble, but who slipped—and don't we all—and reminded us. (My pastor once said to me, aware of my pride in my humility, "The moment you announce you're humble, you no longer are.") This award is also in honor of West's three-piece suit—a nod to W.E.B. Du Bois's Victorian duds—the armor that West slips into every day to fight the good fight. Only problem is, he made a lot of people mad when he said that, generally speaking, black intellectuals these days dress so shabbily. Since most black intellectuals can't pony up for nineteenth century gear—or, for that matter, most twentieth-century high fashion—the only hope is for J.C. Penney to recruit West to design affordable clothes for private intellectuals. (Be careful, though, of all those low-paying sweatshops; they almost ruined TV personality Kathie Lee Gifford's clothing empire.)

THE MOSES "WHO ME? I CAN'T TALK" AWARD. This goes to Robin D.G. Kelley, a New York University historian and cultural critic. He is, without question, one of the most gifted scholars of any generation, of any discipline, of any school, writing today. Kelley is ridiculously well rounded: a gourmet cook, an excellent father, a devoted husband, a committed mentor to graduate students, and an indefatigable researcher and writer. But he won't own up to his gift to clearly explain complex stuff in public. Given all the crap out here (uh, I wasn't referring to my crap), we need Kelley's passionately intelligent voice. To show you what a sacrificial—oops, I mean, helpful—public intellectual I can be, I once reluctantly accepted an assignment that was first offered to Kelley. The second time I appeared on the *Oprah Winfrey* show happened because Kelley turned them down and recommended me. Listen, if it had been anybody but Kelley (not me, mind you, I'm above the fray) the *Oprah* staff could have asked us to speak about birds, and we would have put on some Charlie Parker records, rented a few Tweetie and Sylvester tapes for inspiration, and become an ornithologist overnight. I've got the solution: let's introduce Kelley to R&B sensation R. Kelly. The next time we see him, he'll be known as "R.D.G., That's Kelley you see," and he'll be saying, "I don't see nothin' wrong with a little pub in *Time*."

THE "I'M NOT A PROPHET, BUT I PLAY ONE ON TV" AWARD. This goes to Christians like West, James Cone, and myself, and to those inspired by Buddhist spirituality, like bell hooks. We all use the term "prophet" in one way or another. Although you won't catch us saying so, we sometimes mean it to apply to ourselves. Hold on. Let's be honest here. This probably applies to *all* public intellectuals, who fancy themselves prophets of a sort. We mean well, but hey, I guess we've got to realize that real prophets—of whom there are precious few—lead much more dangerous, sacrificial lives. Don't get me wrong, we've received our share of threats, nasty letters, vile communication, and hateful responses from unhappy readers, viewers, or listeners. And we are, well, deeply sacrificial, and, occasionally, prophetic. But when I think of a prophet like Martin Luther King, Jr., we just don't cut it. He spent his life paying the price for the title. Plus, King made something like two hundred thousand dollars a year in speaking engagements and gave nearly every penny of it to the SCLC, keeping only four thousand to supplement his six thousand a year salary at his church. Black public intellectuals nowadays can make anywhere from a hundred thousand to over a million dollars a year. We say critical things in public, a lot of people hate us for it, we often act brave. But we profit while we prophet.

THE BARBARA MANDRELL "I WAS A PUBLIC INTELLECTUAL WHEN PUBLIC INTELLECTUALS WEREN'T COOL" AWARD. Angela Davis wins this, hands down. A long time ago—when gangsta rappers had the bourgeois blues in their diapers while she was stepping to the revolution; when most celebrated intellectuals were eating their Wheaties, going to Jack and Jill, and courting in the front parlor while she was applying Marcuse to social misery; when more-radical-than-thou critics were enjoying the creature comforts that stoke their dizzy nostalgia for marginality while she was taking three squares in a cramped cell; and when most post-feminists were getting pedicures to put their best foot forward at the debutante while she wore jungle boots at the front line of class warfare—Angela Davis lived what we mean by black public intellectual. She continues to embody that. And she still fine!

THE "EXCUSE THE ACCENT, BUT I'M A WANNA-BEATLES" AWARD. This goes to Paul Gilroy, a black British critic who, in his book, *The Black Atlantic,* has brilliantly forced Americans to think about black identity in an international context. So what's the problem with this latest British invasion? Well, Gilroy just plain trashes most black American intellectuals, often calling us "wrong" for no compelling reason. And for a thinker who spends a lot of time talking about hybridity—meaning that black identity is complex and varied—he completely ignores black American intellectuals who talk about these issues with sophistication and skill. Plus, Gilroy pretty much disses any form of ethnic solidarity, failing to see how that solidarity has often been a means of black survival. After all, black folk weren't oppressed as individuals; we were oppressed because of our group identity.

It's painful to see Gilroy rake black folk over the coals in public lectures. He just doesn't get it. Part of the deference paid to him has to do with his ties to England, a place America still cowers before intellectually. White folk love to hear that colonial accent employed to dog black rappers, public intellectuals, and all the other Negroes who don't measure up. Gilroy may have the black Atlantic down pat; it's the black specific that he needs to bone up on.

THE "HEY, DON'T COMPARE BLACK INTELLECTUALS TO JEWISH INTELLECTUALS, BECAUSE THEY'RE NOT THAT GOOD" AWARD. This award goes to critics William Phillips and Leon Wieseltier. Phillips noted in *Partisan Review* how the New York intellectuals, a large number of whom were Jewish, didn't stoop to the crass, pop cultural stuff that black intellectuals have gained notoriety for. And unlike black intellectuals, Phillips says, Jewish intellectuals weren't obsessed with—in fact, they didn't even talk about—their Jewish ethnicity or about race. And he's bragging about that?

Wieseltier is painfully transparent. His vicious attack on Cornel West in the *New Republic* is a bitter piece of calumny, a screed motivated in large part by jealousy. But Wieseltier's sledgehammer approach to West's work seems to package an even uglier view of the black-Jewish conflict: by setting West up as the premier black intellectual, and then knocking him down, Wieseltier is knocking the black intellectual enterprise in general. He does so, in part, by arguing that West's use of the Hebrew prophets is ill-fated and dim-witted; Wieseltier, in effect, is rescuing sacred Jewish texts and teachers from what he seems to think is West's inferior intelligence.

But those texts and teachers need to be rescued from Wieseltier's nasty grip. After all, the best of Jewish sacred traditions counsels wise, balanced criticism, not the sort of wholesale bludgeoning Wieseltier practices. Although we often forget it, this critical juncture of head and heart is where blacks and Jews can still embrace.

THE "DO AS I SAY, NOT AS I DO" AWARD. This goes to talented Princeton historian Sean Wilentz, who wrote a critique of black public intellectuals in *Dissent*. Really, it was mostly about Cornel West; when he referred to me and bell hooks, it was as "another writer." That little glitch, and Wilentz's commentary, show several things. One, that white folk often choose one black to be the designated hitter, losing sight of other players, reinforcing what Zora Neale Hurston termed the "Pet Negro" system that they despise but help perpetuate. Two, by focusing on one black in what is at least a generational phenomenon, he slights the diversity of opinion, status, and style among black public intellectuals, which allows him to make generalizations that don't hold up under closer investigation.

Three, Wilentz worries that fame, fortune, and celebrity will corrupt black intellectuals. In the attempt to help black public intellectuals avoid such seductions, why wasn't Wilentz writing about black intellectual work a decade ago, before the market mandated it, before celebrity occasioned it? He would then look like a critic motivated by nothing save the best interests of black intellectual life, the academy, and so on. As it stands, he's the big winner. Since writing in *Dissent* (a public intellectual venue) about the pitfalls of too much press and exposure, he's written for the *New Yorker,* an even larger public intellectual organ, and gained more opportunity to express his views in public. I think Wilentz owes black public intellectuals some royalties!

THE "HOOPS AT HARVARD" AWARD. This award goes to Henry Louis Gates, Jr. Skip said he feels like the coach of the Dream Team, luring to Harvard such stars as Cornel West and William Julius Wilson to join team members like K. Anthony Appiah, Evelyn Higginbotham, and Orlando

Patterson. Let's face it, a lot of people are just plain jealous of what Gates—a gifted scholar, writer, and administrator—has been able to do at Harvard: gather big names at an elite institution to think hard and long about the problems black folk face. They have the juice, and some people just can't stand it: they're smart, sharp, sophisticated scholars. They deserve to be on The Team.

The problem comes when it's said like the other places have, well, scrubs, folk that ought to think about retiring or who can only come off the bench, streak scorers who can't really start at their positions. Boy, look at how the metaphor just goes downhill, Skip. Hey, Princeton's team ain't so bad, and neither is Yale's. I hear Michigan's going to the playoffs this year, and that Emory is one of the teams to watch.

Harvard's is a great team, but maybe it's not the Dream Team. Because then Gates would have to explain why David Levering Lewis—arguably the most virtuosic contemporary black intellectual, what with his books on Africa, the Harlem Renaissance, Martin Luther King, Jr., and W.E.B. Du Bois—isn't signed. Or why Nell Painter, a formidable historian of the South, is missing. He'd have to tell us what happened to the erudite Africanist, V.Y. Mudimbe, or the learned historian of religion, Charles Long. Or why the astonishingly smart Patricia Williams isn't suited up in crimson.

Besides, if Harvard's faculty is really the Dream Team, they have an extra burden: they're expected to win the gold every time. More than that, they can't play every pick-up game (conference, television show, lecture appearance, and the like) they're offered. They can't produce sloppy, insubstantial work. They've got to generate serious, thoughtful, well-wrought books and articles.

And if, as West and Gates have repeatedly claimed, the days of HNIC are over, then both have to do a difficult thing:

spread some of the influence and surrender some of the power by which they've managed to affect the careers of other black scholars. Otherwise, saying they don't desire to be HNIC becomes a cover for reinforcing their privileged status.

On the PR front, Skip, you've got to get together with Cornel so he can give you some lessons in Humility 101. (I definitely need to sit in on these as well!) First thing you learn is that from now on you say, "I'm pleased that we're assembling a marvelous collection of scholars here at Harvard. We're certainly not the only place where such good intellectual company may be found, but we're proud to be one of them." Then I'm voting you Coach of the Year. That is, if you can sign Dennis Rodman!

THE PROBLEMS AND POSSIBILITIES of black public intellectuals are huge. We've got a chance to make a difference in the world—something a lot of folk can't say, a chance a lot of scholars don't get. We shouldn't allow pettiness or jealousy to stop us. If black intellectuals keep bickering, bellyaching, and bitterly attacking one another, we'll blow it. And we shouldn't allow the forces and resources of the marketplace to set us against one another. We should be using our minds to shine a light on the real foes of black folk and democracy: poverty, capital flight, right-wing extremists, religious fundamentalists, and the politics of conservatives and neoliberals that hurt the working class and the working poor. Of course, we shouldn't mute our criticisms of black figures, as long as they are just.

Neither should we overlook the limitations of our most treasured black institutions, like the black church. The way that great institution has handled issues of sex, of the body and soul, are terribly important for millions of blacks who look to the church for guidance and inspiration.

THREE

When You Divide Body and Soul, Problems Multiply

The Black Church and Sex

He healed my body, and told me to run on.

Gospel song
"Can't Nobody Do Me Like Jesus"

Love…gives you a good feeling. Something like sanctified.

Marvin Gaye
"Let's Get It On," 1973

Sexual healing is good for me.

Marvin Gaye
"Sexual Healing," 1982

THE VISITING PREACHER, a brawny brown man with smooth skin and teeth made of pearl, was coming to the close of his sermon, a ritual moment of climax in the black church. It is the inevitable point to which the entire service builds. Its existence is the only justification for the less dramatic rites of community—greeting visitors, collecting tithes, praying for the sick, reading scripture, and atoning for sins. These rites are a hallway to the sanctuary of zeal and vision formed by the black sermon. The furious splendor of the preacher's rhythmic, almost sung, speech drove the congregation to near madness. His relentless rhetoric stood them on their feet. Their bodies lurched in holy oblivion to space or time. Their hands waved as they shrieked their assent to the gospel lesson he passionately proclaimed. His cadence quickened. Each word swiftly piled on top of the next. The preacher's sweet moan sought to bring to earth the heavenly light of which his words, even at their most brilliant, were but a dim reflection.

"We've got to keep o-o-o-o-on keepin' on," he tunefully admonished. The preceding wisdom of his oration on Christian sexuality, arguing the link between passion and morality, turned this cliché into a sermonic clincher.

"We can't give up," he continued. "Because we've got God, oh yes, we've got Go-o-o-o-d, um-humh, on our side."

"Yes," members of the congregation shouted. The call and response between the pulpit and the pew escalated as each spurred the other on in ever enlarging rounds of emotion.

"We've got a friend who will never forsake us."

"Yes sir, Reverend."

"We've got a God who can make a way outta no way."

"Yes we do."

"He's a heart fixer, and a mind regulator."

"Oh, yes He is."

"I'm here tonight to tell you whatever moral crisis you're facin', God can fix it for you."

"Thank you, Jesus."

"If you're facin' trouble on the job, God can make your boss act better."

"Tell the truth, Reverend."

"If your kids won't act right, God can turn them around."

"Hallelujah!"

"If you're fornicating, and I know some of y'all been fornicatin', God can turn lust to love and give you a healthier relationship with Him."

"Hold your hope! Hold your hope!"

"If you're committin' adultery, and I know some of y'all are doing that, too, God can stop your rovin' eyes and keep you from messin' up. Won't He do it, church?"

"Yes! Yes He will!"

"If your marriage is fallin' apart, and there's no joy—I said there's no jo-oy-oy-oy—at your address, God can do for you what He did for David. David asked God: 'Restore unto me the joy of Thy salvation.' I'm a witness tonight, children. God can do that, church. God can restore your joy. Won't He do it, children?!"

"Yes He will! Thank you, Jesus! Thank you, Jesus!"

"I'm closin' now, but before I go, I just stopped by to let you know that you can't find salvation in things. You can't find salvation in clothes. You can't find salvation in your car. You can't find salvation in your wife or husband. And you certainly can't find salvation in sex. Did y'all hear me? You can't find salvation in sex. You can't find it in sleepin' around, tryin' to fill the empty places of your life with pleasure and loose livin'."

"Thank you, Jesus!"

"You can only find salvation in our Lord and Savior, Jesus Christ! Do y'all hear me? Jesus, that's who you need! Jesus, that's who can save you. Jesus, the author and finisher of our faith. Jesus! Jesus! Jesus!"

"Thank ya! Oh, hallelujah."

The congregation erupted in waves of shouting and hand-clapping as the minister withdrew from the microphone and dramatically spun to his seat. He was thoroughly spent from a 45-minute exercise in edification and enlightenment. As soon as he was done, his fellow ministers on the dais, including me, descended on the preacher's chair to thank him for his thoughtful, thrilling message. Sex, after all, is a difficult subject to treat in the black church, or, for that matter, in any church. This is indeed ironic. After all, the Christian faith is grounded in the Incarnation, the belief that God took on flesh to redeem human beings. That belief is constantly trumped by Christianity's quarrels with the body. Its needs. Its desires. Its sheer materiality. But especially its sexual identity.

I got a glimpse that night, or, I should say, a reminder, of how deeply ambivalent Christians are about sex. I learned, too, how dishonest we're sometimes made by the unresolved disputes between our bodies and our beliefs.

After the service was over, after the worshipers had time to greet and thank the preacher, we ministers, five in all, retired to the pastor's study.

"Doc, you blessed me tonight," beamed the pastor, a middle-aged preacher of no mean talent himself. (Among black ministers and their circle of intimates, "Doc" or "Doctor" is an affectionate term given to preachers. It began, perhaps, as a way of upgrading the minister to the level of respect his gifts deserved, especially at a time when black ministers were prevented from completing their formal education.)

"Thank you, man," the preacher gently replied with a kind of "aw shucks" smile.

"Yeah, Doctor, you were awful, just terrible, boy," a second minister enthused, heaping on the guest the sort of congratulation black preachers often give to one another.

"Revrun, it was judgment in here tonight," another minister chimed in with yet another line of black preacherly praise. "You killed everythang in here. And if it wasn't dead, you put it in intensive care." At that, we all laughed heartily and agreed that the preacher had hit his mark.

As a young minister in my early twenties, I was just glad to be in their number, bonding with ministerial mentors, men standing on the front line of spiritual warfare, or, as the black church memorably refers to it, "standing in the gap": carrying and crying the judgment of the Almighty, opening opportunity for salvation, proclaiming the soul's rescue and the requirements of redemption, and edifying believers with the inscrutable, wholly uncompromising, tell-it-like-it-is, to-be-preached-in-season-and-out-of-season gospel of the living God. I was simply enjoying this magical moment of fraternal friendliness. And it was just that. No women were there. No one thought it odd that they weren't. We never remarked once on their absence, and, indeed, we counted on their absence to say things, manly things, that we couldn't, didn't dare say, in mixed company. Still, I wasn't prepared for what followed.

"Revrun, I need to ask you something," the visiting preacher begged the pastor. His eyebrows were raised, a knowing look was on his face, and his voice affected, if not quite a mock seriousness, then a naughty whisper that clued us that his curiosity was more carnal than cerebral.

"Who is that woman with those big breasts who was sitting on the third aisle to my left?" he eagerly inquired.

"Damn, she kept shouting and jiggling so much I almost lost my concentration."

"She *is* a fine woman, now," the pastor let on.

"Well, Doc, do you think you could fix me up with her?" the visiting preacher asked with shameless lust.

"I'll see what I can do, Revrun," the pastor promised.

The married preacher's naked desire shocked me. To my surprise, it also made me secretly envious. The fact that he could seek an affair less than an hour after he had thundered against it offended my naive, literal sense of the Christian faith. I thought immediately of how angry I'd been in the past when I heard preachers justify their moral failings, especially their sexual faults. Such ministers chided their followers with a bit of theological doggerel dressed up as a maxim: "God can hit a straight lick with a crooked stick."

But in ways I didn't yet completely understand, I envied the preacher's sense of sexual confidence. He was able to zoom in on his desire and, to borrow a favorite neo-Pentecostal catchphrase, "to name it and claim it." The preacher—and he was surely aware of it, since he didn't let principle stand in the way of his pleasure—had apparently made his peace, however temporary, with the war between Christian ideals and delights of the flesh. I hadn't.

Still, I'm glad I didn't mount a high horse that night to trample the preacher. I've developed enough failures in the sometimes bloody management of erotic desire. So have many other black Christians. Especially those seeking, like most people of faith, to close the gap between what they believe and how they behave. That night, I was nearly tortured by questions I couldn't answer. Was the preacher's theology off? Did he have a flawed understanding of how a Christian should view the body and its sexual urges? Was his extreme sexual libertarianism just plain out of order?

Was he simply a hypocrite? Or was he acting out, however crudely, a confused sense of black Christian sexuality that is, by turns, repressed and excessive? Or all of the above?

The answers to these questions are not as simple as we might believe, despite the rigid certainty of self-anointed arbiters of Christian Truth. And neither are the answers relevant simply for cases, like the one I've described, where everyone can agree that something was wrong. It's much more difficult to figure out how we can have a healthy sense of black Christian sexual identity in a world where being black has been a sin, where black sexuality has been viewed as a pathology, and where the inability to own—and to own up to—our black bodies has led us to devalue our own flesh. We must recover the erotic uses of our bodies from the distortions of white racism and the traps of black exploitation. We must liberate ourselves to embrace the Christian bliss of our black bodies.

At the beginning of the African presence in the New World, black bodies were viewed in largely clinical and capitalist terms. The value of black slave bodies was determined by their use in furthering the reach of Western colonial rule; expanding the market economies of European and American societies; institutionalizing leisure for white cultural elites; deepening the roots of democracy for white property-owning gentry; and providing labor for the material culture that dominates the American landscape. Interestingly, when Christianity poked its nose in, chattel slavery, already a vile and dehumanizing affair, got even uglier.

Christianity insisted there was a need to save the savages from their own cultural deficits. White Christians sought to rescue slaves from perdition by making sure what little soul they had was made suitable for the Kingdom of God. Christianity gave theological legitimacy, and racial justification, to widely held beliefs about black inferiority. It also sanctified the brutal methods deemed necessary to tame the beastly urges of black Africans. White society exploited black labor. White Christianity made it appear that God was behind the whole scheme. Some argued that God used slavery as a tool to bring backward Africans to America. They believed God used white slavers to save black souls by subjugating their bodies. Christian theology shook hands with slavery and sailed off into the sunset of white supremacy.

A key to keeping blacks under white control was the psychological poison pumped into the intellectual diets of slaves. Whites viewed black bodies as ugly, disgusting, and bestial, and blacks were made aware of this. Black bodies were spoken of in the same breath as, say, horses and cows. As if being viewed as an animal wasn't bad enough, blacks were also considered property. Because of Western beliefs about the connection between moral and aesthetic beauty, the belief in the ugliness of black bodies carried over to attitudes about black souls.

Black sexuality sat at the heart of such judgments. If black bodies were demeaned, black sexuality was demonized. Unless, of course, it was linked to breeding black babies for slavery, or, in the case of black women, satisfying the lust of white men. Thus, a central paradox of black sexuality began. Even as whites detested black bodies for their raw animalism, they projected onto those same black bodies their repressed sexual yearnings. Black bodies provided recreational and therapeutic relief for whites. Although that paradox has certainly lessened, it has not entirely disappeared.

For the most part, black sexuality was cloaked in white fantasy and fear. Black women were thought to be hot and ready to be bothered. Black men were believed to have big sexual desires and even bigger organs to realize their lust.

White men became obsessed with containing the sexual threat posed by black men. The competition for white women was mostly mythical. It was largely the projection of white men's guilt for raping black women. Even after slavery, white men beat, burned, hung, and often castrated black men in response to the perceived threat black men represented. White men also repressed white female sexuality by elevating a chaste white womanhood above the lustful reach of black men. Well before gangsta rap, the crotch was the crux of black masculine sexual controversy.

During slavery and after emancipation, blacks both resisted and drank in sick white beliefs about black sexuality. Some blacks sought to fulfill the myth of unquenchable black lust. The logic isn't hard to figure out: if white folk think I'm a sexual outlaw, some blacks perhaps thought, I'll prove it. Other blacks behaved in exactly the opposite fashion. They rigidly disciplined their sexual urges to erase stereotypes of excessive black sexuality. During slavery, many black women resisted sexual domination through abortion, abstinence, and infanticide. They interrupted white pleasure and profit one body at a time.

The rise of the black church, first as an invisible institution and then as the visible womb of black culture, provided a means of both absorbing and rejecting the sexual values of white society. Black religion freed the black body from its imprisonment in crude, racist stereotypes. The black church combated as best it could the self-hatred and the hatred of other blacks that white supremacy encouraged with evil efficiency. It fought racist oppression by becoming the headquarters of militant social and political action in black communities. The black church produced leaders who spoke with eloquence and prophetic vigor about the persistence of white racism. It was the educational center of black communities, supporting colleges that trained blacks who became shock troops in the battle for racial equality. Black churches unleashed the repressed forces of cultural creativity and religious passion. The church also redirected black sexual energies into the sheer passion and emotional explosiveness of its worship services.

I'm certainly not saying, as do those who argue that black religion compensates for racial oppression—we can't beat up the white man so we cut up in church—that the displacement of black sexual energy by itself shaped black worship. I'm simply suggesting that the textures, styles, and themes of black worship owe a debt to a complicated sexual history. In sharp contrast to the heat of most black worship experiences, there emerged almost immediately in black churches a conservative theology of sexuality. In part, this theology reflected the traditional teachings of white Christianity. Out of moral necessity, however, black Christians exaggerated white Christianity's version of "p.c."— Puritan Correctness. Later, many black Christians adopted white Christianity's Victorian repression to rebut the myth of black sexuality being out of control.

The contemporary black church still reflects the roots of its unique history. It continues to spawn social action, though not on the same fronts as it once did. The increased secularization of black communities, and the rise of political leadership outside of the black church, has blunted the focus of the church's prophetic ministry. Some things, however, have changed very little. There remains deeply entrenched in black churches a profoundly conservative theology of sexuality. Like all religious institutions where doctrine is questioned, rejected, perhaps even perverted by members, the black church faces a tense theological situation. Unlike, say, the Catholic or Episcopal church where an elaborate and more unyielding hierarchy prevails, historically black churches have a real opportunity to bring lasting change more quickly to their religious bodies. Such change is sorely needed in black communities and churches where issues of sexuality have nearly exploded.

Of course, there are problems that are easily identified but are difficult to solve. Earlier and earlier, black boys and girls are becoming sexually active. Teen pregnancy continues to escalate. Besides these problems, there are all sorts of sexual challenges that black Christians face. The sexual exploitation of black female members by male clergy. The guilt and shame that result from unresolved conflicts about the virtues of black sexuality. The continued rule of black churches by a mainly male leadership. The role of eroticism in a healthy black Christian sexuality. The revulsion to and exploitation of homosexuals. The rise of AIDS in black communities. The sexual and physical abuse of black women and children by black male church members. The resistance to myths of super black sexuality. And the split between mind and body that leads to confusion about a black Christian theology of Incarnation. What should be done?

For starters, the black church should build on a celebration of the body in black culture and worship. Ours, quite simply, is a body-centered culture. Sharp criticism by black intellectuals, including me, of essentialism—the idea that there is such a thing as black culture's essence, and that we get at it by viewing blacks as a monolith, ignoring differences made by region, sexuality, gender, class, and the like— has made many critics reluctant to highlight persistent features of black life. But in many African and black American communities, colorful, creative uses of the body prevail. (Unfortunately, as we have learned with resurgent slavery and genital mutilation of females in Africa, destructive and oppressive uses of the body mark our cultures as well.) Many black folk use vibrant, sometimes flamboyant, styles and colors to adorn their bodies. Johnnie Cochran's purple suit and Dennis Rodman's weirdly exotic hairstyles and body tattoos reveal a flare for outrageous, experimental fashion. Plus, the styling of black bodies for creative expression—Michael Jordan's gravity-rattling acrobatics, singer Anita Baker's endearing tics, Denzel Washington's smoothly sensuous gait, and Janet Jackson's brilliant integration of street and jazz dance—underscores the improvisational uses of black bodies.

The black church, too, is full of beautiful, boisterous, burdened, and brilliant black bodies in various stages of praising, signifying, testifying, shouting, prancing, screaming, musing, praying, meditating, singing, whooping, hollering, prophesying, preaching, dancing, witnessing, crying, faking, marching, forgiving, damning, exorcising, lying, confessing, surrendering, and overcoming. There is a relentless procession, circulation, and movement of black bodies in the black church: the choir gliding in and grooving to the rhythmic sweep of a grinding gospel number; members marching aisle by aisle to plop a portion of their earnings in the collection plate; women sashaying to the podium to deliver the announcements; kids huddling around the teacher for the children's morning message; the faithful standing at service's start to tell how good the Lord's been to them this week; the convicted leaping to their feet to punctuate a preacher's point in spiritual relief or guilt; the deliberate saunter to the altar of the "whosoever wills" to pray for the sick and bereaved, and for themselves; the white-haired, worldly-wise deacon bowing down at his seat to thank God that he was spared from death, that "the walls of my room were not the walls of my grave," his bed "sheet was not my winding sheet," and his bed was not "my cooling board"; the church mother shaking with controlled chaos as the Holy Ghost rips straight through her vocal cords down to her abdomen; the soloist's hands gesturing grandly as she bends each note into a rung on Jacob's ladder to carry the congregation "higher and higher"; the ushers' martial precision as they gracefully guide guests to a spot where they might get a glimpse of glory; the choir director calling for pianissimo with a guileless "shhhh" with one hand as the other directs the appointed soprano to bathe the congregation in her honey-sweet "ha-lay-loo-yuh"; and the preacher, the magnificent center of rhetorical and ritualistic gravity, fighting off disinterest with a "you don't hear me," begging for verbal response by looking to the ceiling and drolly declaring "amen lights," twisting his body to reach for "higher ground," stomping the floor, pounding the pulpit, thumping the Bible, spinning around, jumping pews, walking benches, climbing ladders—yes literally—opening doors, closing windows, discarding robes, throwing bulletins, hoisting chairs, moaning, groaning, sweating, humming, chiding, pricking, and edifying, all to better "tell the story of Jesus and his love." In the black church, it's all about the body: the saved and sanctified body, the fruitful and faithful body, working and waiting for the Lord.

The body, too, is at the center of what Christian theologians have long termed the "scandal of particularity": the very idea that an unlimited, transcendent God would become a human being, time-bound and headed for death, was just too hard for nonbelievers to swallow. That scandal has special relevance for black Christians, who draw courage from a God who would dare sneak into human history as a lowly, suffering servant. From the plantation to the postindustrial city, suffering blacks have readily identified with a God who, they believe, first identified with them.

The black church has helped blacks find a way to overcome pain, to live through it, to get around it, and, finally, to prosper in spite of it. Black religion has often encouraged black folk to triumph over tragedy by believing that undeserved suffering could be turned to good use. That idea sparked the public ministry of Martin Luther King, Jr., a towering son of the black church. The radical identification with Jesus' life and death, which happened, after all, in his body, has permitted black Christians to endure the absurd violence done to their bodies. Through church sacraments, black Christians nurtured and relieved their bodies' suffering memories. On every first Sunday of the month, or whenever they celebrated the Lord's Supper, black Christians broke bread and drank wine, knowing that Jesus' crucified body was their crucified body, and that Jesus' resurrected body could be theirs as well. Every time the words of Holy Communion were repeated, "this do in remembrance of me," black Christians remembered those lost warriors who once fought mightily against oppression but who now slept with the ancestors.

Above all, the Incarnation revealed to black folk a God who, when it came to battling impossible odds, had been there and done that. Because black Christians inevitably had to pass through the "valley of the shadow of death," they could take solace from a God who had faced a host of ills they faced. Divine abandonment. Cruel cursing. Ethnic bigotry. Religious marginalization. Unjust punishment. Spiteful epithets. And most important, vicious death. Just knowing that God had walked this same earth, eaten this same food, tasted this same disappointment, experienced this same rejection, fought this same self-doubt, endured this same betrayal, felt this same isolation, encountered this same opposition, and overcome this same pain often made the difference between black folk living and dying.

It is INDEED IRONIC THAT, with so much staked on the body, many black Christians continue to punish themselves with the sort of extreme self-denial that has little to do with healthy sexuality. To a large extent, the black church has aimed to rid the black body of lascivious desires and to purge its erotic imagination with "clean" thoughts. All the while, the black worship experience formed the erotic body of black religious belief, with all the rites of religious arousal that accompany sexual union.

Indeed, the story of the visiting minister that begins this chapter portrays the erotic intensity of the black worship experience: the electric call-and-response between minister and congregation; the fervent temper of the preacher's words of wisdom and warning; the extraordinary effort by the minister to seduce the audience onto God's side through verbal solicitation; and the orgasmic eruption of the congregation at the end of the sermon. It requires no large sophistication to tell that something like sexual stimulation was going on.

Perhaps that's because there is a profound kinship between spirituality and sexuality. Great mystics figured that out a long time ago. More recently, so have black singers Marvin Gaye, the artist formerly known as Prince, and R. Kelly. Black Christians are reluctant to admit the connection because we continue to live in Cartesian captivity: the mind-body split thought up by philosopher Descartes flourishes in black theologies of sexuality. Except it is translated as the split between body and soul. Black Christians have taken sexual refuge in the sort of rigid segregation they sought to escape in the social realm—the body and soul in worship are kept one place, the body and soul in heat are kept somewhere else. That's ironic because, as critic Michael Ventura has argued, black culture, especially black music, has healed, indeed transcended, the split between mind and body inherited from Descartes and certain forms of Christian theology. Segments of secular black culture have explored the intimate bond of sexuality and spirituality. The black church has given a great deal to black culture, including the style and passion of much of black pop music. It is time the church accepted a gift in return: the union of body and soul.

The sensuality of our bodies must be embraced in worship. That sensuality should be viewed as a metaphor for the passion of our sexual relations as well. And vice versa. The link between sexuality and spirituality was hinted at when the Bible talked of the church as Christ's bride, and alternately, as the body of Christ. Because Christian belief is rooted in the Incarnation, in the body, Anglican theologian William Temple held that Christianity is literally the most material of all religions. The sheer materiality of our faith is not simply a protection against those versions of Christianity that get high on the soul's salvation and forget about the body's need to eat. It is also a rebuke to those who believe that God is opposed to our sexual pleasure. To twist literary critic Roland Barthes, we should celebrate the pleasure of the text, especially when the text is, literally, our bodies.

Simply put, the black church needs a theology of eroticism. Admittedly, that is a hard sell in an Age of Epidemic, where panic and paranoia, more than liberty and celebration, set our sexual moods. Of course, black sexuality has always thrived or suffered under a permanent sign of suspicion or revulsion. Still, that's no reason to be cavalier about sex when its enjoyment can kill us. A theology of eroticism certainly promotes safe sex. Our definition of safety, however, must include protection against the harmful sexual *and* psychic viruses that drain the life from our desire. Further, a theology of eroticism looks beyond the merely physical to embrace abstinence as a powerful expression of sexuality.

In the main, a theology of eroticism must be developed to free black Christian sexuality from guilty repression or gutless promiscuity. Sermon after sermon counsels black Christians to abstain from loose behavior. To sleep only with our mates. To save sex for permanent love. And to defer sexual gratification until we are married. In black churches, as with most religious institutions, hardly anyone waits for marriage to have sex. People sleep with their neighbor's spouse. Casual sex is more than casually pursued. And because the needs of their bodies make them liars with bad consciences, some drown their demons in a sea of serial monogamies. Little of this is highly pleasurable, but it's pleasurable enough to make us unhappy. Ugh!

What's even more intriguing is that the sermons pretty much stay the same. Black Christians pretty much tell their children and each other that that's how things ought to be. And consistency is seen as a substitute for tradition. But it certainly isn't. Vital, living traditions leave space for people to change bad habits because they have a better understanding of what the tradition should mean. As one wise churchman put it: *tradition* is the living faith of dead people, while the *traditional* is the dead faith of living people. Too often, the latter has ruled black churches. While we may share our forebears' faith, we can certainly leave aspects of their theologies behind.

A theology of eroticism is rooted in simple honesty about black sexuality. While we tell our kids not to have sex, more and more of them do. They are making babies, having babies, and dying from AIDS. The black church should lay off the hard line on teen sexuality. Sure, it must preach abstinence first. It should also preach and teach safe sex, combining condoms and common sense. It should tell kids from ages twelve through seventeen that when it's all said and done, human sexuality is still an enlarging mystery, a metaphor of how life seeks more of itself to sustain itself, of how life, as black theologian Howard Thurman remarked, is itself alive. (Of course, we adults could use a reminder of this as well.) Our sexuality is one way life reminds itself of that lesson. In the hands of groping teens, sex is often little more than bewilderment multiplied by immaturity, despite growing, groaning body parts that seem fit for the job. In an era when music videos, television commercials, daytime soaps, and nighttime cable movies exploit our kids' urges, it's no wonder that they, and indeed, all of us, have sex on the brain. If only we could use *that* organ more in our erotic escapades.

The bottom line, however, is that traditional black church methods of curbing teen sex aren't working. We must make a choice. Either we counsel our kids about how to have sex as safely as they can, or we prepare to bury them before their lives begin. The cruelty of contemporary sex is that the consequences of our kids' mistakes, the same mistakes we made, are often swift and permanent. Most black preachers and parents who tell kids they shouldn't have sex had sex as teens. If not, most of them surely tasted carnal pleasure before they were married. The guilt or embarrassment stirred by their hidden hypocrisy often makes them harsh and unyielding in their views on teen sexuality. The black church's theology of eroticism should place a premium on healthy, mature relations where lust is not mistaken for affection. It must make allowances for our children, however, to learn the difference, and to safely experiment with their bodies in pursuit of genuine erotic health. The black church should pass out condoms on its offering plates. At the least, it should make them available in restrooms or in the offices of clergypersons or other counselors. The days of let's-pretend-the-problems-will-go-away, never-fully-here-anyway, are now most certainly gone.

We must find remedies, too, for angst-ridden black preachers. Many of them stir anxiety in their congregations because of their own conflicted theology of sexuality. The visiting minister I spoke of earlier was bewitched by the erotic double-bind that traps some ministers. He preached a theology of sexuality that satisfied the demands of black church tradition. But he was also moved by erotic desires that are rarely openly discussed in black churches, or in the seminaries that prepare men and women to pastor. The sexual exploitation of black women by black preachers, and the seduction of preachers by female members, rests on just this sort of confusion. (Of course, it also rests on a gender hierarchy in black churches where women do much of the labor but are largely prevented from the highest leadership role: the pastorate. The *ecclesiastical apartheid* of the black church, which is more than 70 percent female, continues to reinforce the sexual inequality of black women.) In many cases, both parties are caught in the thralls of unfocused erotic desire. Such desire doesn't receive reasonable, helpful attention. It is either moralized against or it lands on the wagging tongues of church gossips.

As a very young pastor—I was all of 23 years old—I sometimes participated in the sort of sex play that mocks healthy erotic desire. Once, after assuming the pastorate of a small church in the South, I received a call from a desperate female parishioner.

"Reverend Dyson, I need to see you right away," the soft, teary voice on my phone insisted. "It's an emergency. I can't discuss it on the telephone."

It was seven o'clock at night. Since I lived nearly a hundred miles from the city where my church was located, it would take me at least an hour-and-a-half to reach her home.

"Alright, Ms. Bright (not her real name)," I replied. "I'll be there as soon as I can."

I told my fiancée Brenda, with whom I was living, that a member needed me to come immediately. I tore up the highway in a frantic race to Ms. Bright's home. I was a young, relatively inexperienced pastor, new on the job, and eager to please. When I arrived at Ms. Bright's home, her parents greeted me at the door. Judging by the surprised look on their faces, her parents had no idea of their daughter's distress, or her urgent request to see me. When she appeared a few minutes later, I didn't let on that I'd just zoomed to their house to help relieve their daughter of whatever problem she had. To them, I guess it looked like I had come courting on the sly. After all, neither of us were married, and Ms. Bright was only a few years older than me. Although I was in a committed relationship with Brenda, my members didn't know that we were, as the '70s R&B hit goes, "living together in sin." (Already living in the Bible Belt, perhaps on its buckle, I was caught in the crossfire between sex and soul almost before my career as a pastor began.)

Ms. Bright suggested that we go upstairs to her room to talk. We excused ourselves from pleasant chitchat with her amiable parents. We soon found ourselves alone in her stylish, sweetly scented bedroom. I felt awkward. I'd never spent time alone with her before outside of the few occasions we spoke in church. Besides, I didn't know what signal my presence in her boudoir might send. But I soon found out what was weighing on her heart and mind.

"Reverend Dyson, I think I'm in love with you," she blurted out.

I was genuinely startled. I had never been a Don Juan. And despite the crude stereotypes of ministers as lotharios out to bed every woman within speaking distance, I certainly hadn't been promiscuous. I could count the number of girlfriends I'd had on one hand. And I'd never been led to think of myself as irresistibly handsome. I wasn't a guy, like many I'd known, for whom women seemed to pant and pine. I was just Mike Dyson, the poor kid from Detroit who worked hard, studied long, and mostly lived out his sexual fantasies with a few beautiful women.

"Well, Ms. Bright, I, um, I, well, I'm very flattered," I barely managed. By now my yellow face was flushed and my eyes were boring holes in the floor. "I don't know what to say."

Then it hit me. My pastor, Frederick Sampson, knowing that the advice would one day come in handy, had given me a stern warning.

"Never let a woman down harshly, Mike," Dr. Sampson said. "Always be gentle and considerate." Eureka! Here was my out.

"You know, Ms. Bright, what you've said makes me feel good," I uttered with more conviction. "I'm truly honored that a woman like you would even be interested in me. But you know I'm in love with Brenda."

I saw the disappointment in her eyes. Quickly extending Sampson's rule, I was determined not to make Ms. Bright feel foolish.

"But if I was available, you're the kind of woman I would definitely like to be with."

And I wasn't just blowing smoke, as they say. Ms. Bright was a very intelligent, inquisitive woman, as our few conversations revealed. She was also a beautiful woman; a tall five feet ten inches, she dwarfed my five-foot-nine-inch frame. She had flawless chocolate skin, an incandescent smile, a sensuous voice, and a voluptuous figure.

"Really?" she replied.

In retrospect, I guess that gave her an opening. And despite denying it then, I probably wanted her to find it. Although each of us had been sitting on chairs in her room, Ms. Bright stood up and, well, descended on me. Standing directly above me, she confessed that she'd spent a great deal of time daydreaming about me.

"I just can't get you off my mind," she said. "I really think I'm in love with you, Reverend Dyson. I don't know what I'm going to do."

As the words rolled off her tongue, which I began to notice more and more, she began to run her fingers through my hair. I was embarrassed, ashamed, almost mortified—and extremely turned on.

"Well, I don't know either, Ms. Bright," I muttered. "I guess, well, I don't know, I guess we'll just have to…"

Before I could finish, she was kissing me. Before long, we were kissing each other. Our tongues dueled with more energy than we'd been able to devote to resolving her problem. Except now, it was our problem. I wasn't in love with her, but my lust was certainly piqued. Talk about not letting a woman down roughly; I certainly wasn't flunking that test. But I felt bad for cheating on Brenda. I yanked myself free from Ms. Bright's luscious lip-lock and came up for air, reaching as well for a little perspective.

"Look, Ms. Bright, I didn't mean for this to happen," I said through my heavy breathing. "After all, I'm your pastor, and I should be counseling you, not trying to get down with you."

She simply smiled. Then, before I could protest, she was out of her blouse. Next her bra fell to the floor! The queenly, regal pose she struck, part Pam Grier and part British royalty, made me feel like a lowly subject. And gawking at the sheer magnificence of her breasts, I was glad to be in her majesty's service. We groped each other like high-school teens stranded in a hormonal storm. After nearly a half-hour of this pantomimed intimacy, guilt suddenly overtook me. Better yet, the thought of having sex with her parents able to hear the bed creak and groan quenched my erotic fire. I recovered what little pastoral authority I had left—I think it was mixed up with my jacket and tie on the floor—and insisted that we quit. So we fixed up our clothes. Ms. Bright retouched her makeup, and without saying much—what could we say?—we went back downstairs to make small talk with her parents. After fifteen minutes or so, I bid them farewell and drove home far more slowly than I'd driven to my appointment. I was more disappointed at myself than angry at Ms. Bright. Despite what she said—and even she probably didn't really believe it—I didn't think Ms. Bright was in love with me. She simply had a crush, though, admittedly, it was a big one. Plus, she had a healthy dose of sexual desire, a subject we should have been able to talk about, not only in her house but in our church. We should have been able to refer to sex education classes, sermon series, Sunday-school discussions, Sunday-night forums, and a host of other ways that erotic desire might be addressed in the black church. Some churches are doing this, but they are far, far too few in number.

I was flattered that Ms. Bright wanted me. At the same time, I was ashamed that I'd given in to wanting her. I'd come to pray. I'd ended up the prey—the willing prey, as it turned out. Maybe Ms. Bright had seen the desire in my eyes, which failed to be disguised as pastoral concern. Maybe she was simply the first to act on what she knew we both wanted. Maybe she was just more honest.

On my way home, I couldn't help thinking of the visiting preacher. I got a lot more humble. Still, I kept thinking about my erotic encounter with Ms. Bright. Despite trying to feel bad about it, I found myself getting aroused all over again. I hadn't yet figured out that it's alright to enjoy erotic desire—to own up to the fact that you can be horny and holy—as long as you don't live at the mercy of your hormones. But if we can't talk about sex at home, and we can't talk about it at church, black Christians end up lying to ourselves and to the people to whom we're sexually attracted. And too often, we end up being much more destructive because of our erotic dishonesty.

BECAUSE SO MANY BLACK CHRISTIANS have taken up the task of being sexual saviors—of crucifying the myths of black hypersexuality and sexual deviance—we abhor out-of-bounds sexuality. This social conservatism expresses itself as a need to be morally upright. Beyond reproach. (Unsurprisingly, gangsta rappers are high on the list of sinners. If its detractors actually ever listened to more than snippets of gangsta rap lyrics, they'd probably have a lot more grist for their critical mills.) Oh, if it was only that simple. If the black church—for God's sake, if *any* religious institution—was erotically honest, it would admit that the same sexual desire that courses through rappers' veins courses through the veins of its members. If many of the black ministers who wail against the sexual improprieties of hip-hop culture would be erotically honest, they'd admit that the same lust they nail rappers for breaks out in their own ranks. And there aren't too many sermons pointing that out.

The standard religious response has been: "Of course we have the same desires, but we fight them and put them in proper perspective." That's partly true. The desire is certainly fought. Why, you can see the strain of erotic repression on unmade-up faces, in long dresses that hide flesh, and in the desexualized carriage of bodies (notice the burden is largely on the women) in the most theologically rigid of orthodox black churches. But that's just the point: mere repression is not the proper perspective. We've got to find a mean between sexual annihilation and erotic excess. Otherwise, the erotic practices of church members will continue to be stuck in silence and confusion.

Neither are there many sermons that assail ministers for exploiting women. To be sure, there are women who think they were put on earth to please the pastor. For them, embracing his flesh is like embracing a little bit of heaven. Pastors should study their books on transference and help spread light on this fallacy. Of course, there are just as many women who simply get in heat over a man who can talk, especially if they've dealt with men for whom saying hello in the morning is an effort. So let's not romanticize the put-upon, helpless female who's charmed by the wiles of the slick, Elmer Gantry–like, minister-as-omnicompetent-stud-and-stand-in-for-God.

Too often, though, there are women who come to the minister seeking a helping hand who get two instead. Plus some lips, legs, arms—well, you get the picture. The black church is simply running over with brilliant, beautiful black women of every age, hue, and station. Pecan publicists.

Ebony lawyers. Caramel doctors. Mocha engineers. Beige clerks. Bronze businesswomen. Brown housewives. Redbone realtors. Yellow laborers. Coffee teachers. Blueblack administrators. Copper maids. Ivory tellers. Chocolate judges. Tan students. Often these women are sexually pursued by the church's spiritual head, so to speak.

This fact makes it especially hard to endure the chiding of black preachers, veiled in prophetic language, launched at the sexual outlaws of black pop culture. In reality, the great Martin Luther King, Jr., is the patron saint of the sexual unconscious of many black ministers, but for all the wrong reasons. For most of the time he lived in the glare of international fame, King, as is well known, carried on affairs with many women. He wasn't proud of it. He confessed his guilt. He said he'd try to do better. But he just couldn't give it up. Plus, he was away from home for 28 days of most months. Lest too many critics aiming to bring King down a notch or two for his moral failings get any ideas, bear in mind that he spent that kind of time away from his wife and children, under enormous stress and at great peril to his life, leading the war against racial inequality.

Many black ministers have absorbed King's erotic habits, and those of many white and black ministers before and after him. But they have matched neither his sacrifice nor his achievements. Not that such factors excuse King's behavior. But they do help us understand the social pressures that shaped King's erotic choices. One must remember, too, the ecology of erotic expression for civil rights workers. The wife of a famous civil rights leader once told me civil rights workers often went to towns where their presence reviled whites and upset many complacent blacks. She said it was natural that they sexually fed off of each other within their tight circles of sympathy and like-minded perspective. That squares as well with King's comment that a lot of his philandering was a release from the extraordinary pressures he faced. That's probably a large part of the story, though it can't be the complete story. King's behavior apparently predates his fame. His philandering was a complex matter.

In some senses, King's erotic indiscretions were the expression of a Casanova complex, pure and simple. That complex is especially present in famous men whose success is a gateway to erotic escapades. Indeed, their fame itself is eroticized. Their success is both the capital and the commodity of sex. It procures sexual intimacy and is the gift procured by (female) sexual surrender. Then, too, for black men there is a tug-of-war occurring on the psychosexual battlefield. Black men occupy a symbolic status as studs. That stereotype is one of the few that black men refuse to resist. They embrace it almost in defiance of its obvious falseness, as an inside joke. (How many times did King tell white audiences that blacks wanted to be their brothers, not their brothers-in-law, even as white women flaunted themselves before him? King was even set to marry a white woman when he was in seminary, but she was sent away, and King was warned by a mentor that he would never be able to be a black leader with a white wife.)

There is also a specific psychology of the ministerial Casanova. He believes he merits sexual pleasure because of his sacrificial leadership of the church community. Ironically, he sees the erotic realm as an arena of fulfillment because it is forbidden, a forbiddance that he makes a living preaching to others. (Yes, the cliché is certainly true that "That which is denied becomes popular.") But erotic forbiddance is a trap. The very energy exerted against erotic adventure becomes a measure for ministerial integrity. It becomes the very force the minister must resist if he is to be erotically honest. Erotic desire both induces guilt in the minister and is his reward for preaching passionately about the need for the denial of erotic exploitation! Self-delusion and self-centeredness mingle in this arena of sexual desire.

All of this sets up an erotic gamesmanship between minister and the potential—often willing—object of his erotic desire. One of the rules of the game is, "Let's see if I can get him to fall, to act against what he proclaims as truth." This is more than simply a case of Jezebel out to seduce the minister. It is a case of erotic desire being expressed in a way that reflects the unequal relation between male leaders and female followers.

Many ministers who travel on the revival circuit—delivering sermons and giving a lift to the sagging spirits of churches across the nation—too often settle into comfortable habits of sexual exploitation. Their regimen of erotic enjoyment gets locked in early in their careers. They travel to churches, preach the gospel, meet a woman or women, have sex, return home, go back the next year and do the same. Even ministers who stay in place can roam their congregations, or the congregations of their peers, in search of erotic adventure. What it comes down to is that the Martin Luther King, Jrs., and the Snoop Doggy Doggs of black culture all want the same thing. The Snoops are up front about it. Most of us in the black church aren't.

The same erotic dishonesty applies to another sexual identity: homosexuality. The notorious homophobia of the black church just doesn't square with the numerous same-sex unions taking place, from the pulpit to the pew. One of the most painful scenarios of black church life is repeated Sunday after Sunday with little notice or collective outrage. A black minister will preach a sermon railing against sexual ills, especially homosexuality. At the close of the sermon, a soloist, who everybody knows is gay, will rise to perform a moving number, as the preacher extends an invitation to visitors to join the church. The soloist is, in effect, being asked to sing, and to sign, his theological death sentence. His presence at the end of such a sermon symbolizes a silent endorsement of the preacher's message. Ironically, the presence of his gay Christian body at the highest moment of worship also negates the preacher's attempt to censure his presence, to erase his body, to deny his legitimacy as a child of God. Too often, the homosexual dimension of eroticism remains cloaked in taboo or blanketed in theological attack. As a result, the black church, an institution that has been at the heart of black emancipation, refuses to unlock the oppressive closet for gays and lesbians.

One of the most vicious effects of the closet is that some of the loudest protesters against gays and lesbians in the black church are secretly homosexual. In fact, many, many preachers who rail against homosexuality are themselves gay. Much like the anti-Semitic Jew, the homophobic gay or lesbian Christian secures his or her legitimacy in the church by denouncing the group of which he or she is a member, in this case an almost universally despised sexual identity. On the surface, such an act of self-hatred is easy. But it comes at a high cost. Homophobic rituals of self-hatred alienate the gay or lesbian believer from his or her body in an ugly version of erotic Cartesianism: splitting the religious mind from the homosexual body as a condition of Christian identity. This erotic Cartesianism is encouraged when Christians mindlessly repeat about gays and lesbians, "we love the sinner but we hate the sin." A rough translation is "we love you but we hate what you do." Well, that mantra worked with racists: we could despise what racist whites did while refusing to despise white folk themselves, or whiteness per se. (Of course, there were many blacks who blurred that distinction and hated white folk as well as they pleased.) But with gay and lesbian identity, to hate what they do is to hate who they are. Gays and lesbians are how they have sex. (I'm certainly not reducing gay or lesbian identity to sexual acts. I'm simply suggesting that the sign of homosexual difference, and hence the basis of their social identification, is tied to the role of the sex act in their lives.)

The black church must develop a theology of homoeroticism, a theology of queerness. (Well, if we want to be absolutely campy, we might term it a theology for *Afriqueermericans.*) After all, if any group understands what it means to be thought of as queer, as strange, as unnatural, as evil, it's black folk. A theology of queerness uses the raw material of black social alienation to build bridges between gay and lesbian and straight black church members. The deeply entrenched cultural and theological bias against gays and lesbians contradicts the love ethic at the heart of black Christianity. Virulent homophobia mars the ministry of the black church by forcing some of our leading lights into secret and often self-destructive sexual habits. James Cleveland, considered the greatest gospel artist of the contemporary black church, died several years ago, it is rumored, from AIDS. Aside from embarrassed whispers and unseemly gossip, the black church still hasn't openly talked about it. Perhaps if gay and lesbian black church members could come out of their closets, they could leave behind as well the destructive erotic habits that threaten their lives.

The black church should affirm the legitimacy of homoerotic desire by sanctioning healthy unions between consenting gay and lesbian adults. After all, promiscuity, not preference, eats away at the fabric of our erotic integrity. Are gays and lesbians who remain faithful to their partners committing a greater sin than married heterosexuals who commit adultery? The ridiculousness of such a proposition calls for a radical rethinking of our black Christian theology of sexuality.

Central to the doctrine of Incarnation in the black church is the belief that God identified with the most despised members of our society by becoming the most despised member of our society. Sunday after Sunday, black ministers invite us to imagine God as, say, a hobo, or a homeless person. Well, imagine God as gay. Imagine God as lesbian. Is the gay or lesbian body of God to be rejected? Better still, isn't God's love capable of redeeming a gay or lesbian person? The traditional black theological answer has been yes, if that person is willing to "give up" his or her sin—in this case, being gay or lesbian—and turn to God. But a more faithful interpretation of a black theology of love and liberation asserts that God takes on the very identity that is despised or scorned—being black, say, or being poor, or being a woman—to prove its worthiness as a vehicle for redemption. We don't have to stop being black to be saved. We don't have to stop being women to be saved. We don't have to stop being poor to be saved. And we don't have to stop being gay or lesbian to be saved. Black Christians, who have been despised and oppressed for much of our existence, should be wary of extending that oppression to our lesbian sisters and gay brothers.

The black church continues to occupy the center of black culture. Although most black folk have never officially joined its ranks, the influence of the black church spreads far beyond its numbers. The black church raised up priests to administer healing to wounded spirits in slavery.

It produced prophets to declare the judgment of God against racial injustice. The black church has been at the forefront of every major social, political, and moral movement in black culture. It remains our most precious institution. It has the opportunity to lead again, by focusing the black erotic body in its loving, liberating lens. A daughter of the black community, Jocelyn Elders, attempted to bring the sharp insight and collective wisdom of our tradition to a nation unwilling to ponder its self-destructive sexual habits. Let's hope that her advice won't be lost on those closer to home. Like Marvin Gaye, black churches and communities need sexual healing. If we get healed, we might just be able to help spread that health beyond our borders.

Our youth could use a strong dose of that healing. Too often, though, black nostalgia for how we think things used to be for black folk dries up our compassion and sympathy for our youth. But we've got to find our way back into their heads. And we've got to let them back into our hearts. It will take both old and young hashing out our differences, and reaffirming our similarities, as we embrace across the chasm of age and perception. If we don't, we'll have bigger troubles than the ones we already face.

FOUR

We Never Were
What We Used to Be

*Black Youth, Pop Culture,
and the Politics of Nostalgia*

*Our present obsession with the past has the
double advantage of making new work seem
raw and rough compared to the cosy patina of
tradition, whilst refusing tradition its vital connection to what is happening now. By making
islands of separation out of the unbreakable
chain of human creativity, we are able to set up
false comparisons, false expectations, all the
while lamenting that the music, poetry, painting, prose, performance art of Now, fails to live
up to the art of Then, which is why, we say,
it does not affect us. In fact, we are no more
moved by a past we are busy inventing, than by
a present we are busy denying.*

Jeanette Winterson
"Art Objects," 1995

I WASN'T EXPECTING THE REBUFF. Its severity underscored the bitterness of the debate that has formed around urban black youth and the cultures they create.

I had just finished testifying before the United States Senate Judiciary Committee's Subcommittee on Juvenile Justice. Illinois Senator Carol Moseley-Braun, along with Maine Senator William Cohen and Wisconsin Senator and Subcommittee Chair Herbert Kohl, had called the hearing in 1994 to discuss "violent and demeaning imagery in popular music." Predictably, the hearings focused on gangsta rap. While he wasn't within barking distance, rapper Snoop Doggy Dogg was the shadow figure and rhetorical guest of dishonor at the proceedings. His body of work—like the rapper himself, slim but menacingly attractive—was relentlessly attacked by many of the hearing's witnesses. Snoop was made to appear like hip-hop's Mephistopheles, seducing black children to trade their souls for the corrupt delights of "G-funk." The latter is a jeep-rattling, bass-heavy, ripinvention (yes, a mix of ripping off and reinventing) of 1970s funk. Except Snoop and G-funk impresario Dr. Dre's brand of funk is fused to the gangsterish fantasies of 1990s West Coast black youth culture. After having my say—that the music and its artists are complex, that they must be understood in both their cultural and racial setting even as we criticize their hateful sentiments—I was accosted by another witness's husband.

"Don't you have a Ph.D. from Princeton?" the tall, brown-skinned man brusquely quizzed me.

"Yes, sir, I do," I replied.

"And aren't you a Baptist preacher?" he asked, with even more scorn.

"Yes, sir, I am," I said.

"You know, for somebody who's supposed to be so smart, you sure are a dumb ass."

At that, he turned and walked off. He had the kind of self-satisfaction that only proud indignity can conjure. (To be honest, my Detroit homeboy roots nearly cracked the surface of my scholarly and preacherly gentility. But since my mama taught me to respect my elders, I kept my mouth shut.)

There were other times, too, when I caught a glimpse of the hostility between black youth culture and its older critics. Soon after my Washington witnessing, I lectured at Harvard on Malcolm X, ending with a recitation of NWA's (Niggaz With Attitude) rap, "F___ Tha Police." After my talk, a seasoned graduate student approached me, I thought, to praise my performance.

"Your lecture was good, man," he duly noted. "But why would you end by surrendering the nobility of black folk to that barbaric nonsense?"

At still another conference, this time at Princeton, I interjected a long snatch from Snoop's syncopated soliloquy on his and Dr. Dre's rap, "Nothin' But a G Thang." A colleague later reported that a few of the Ivy League's stuffier types found my juxtaposing of Ralph Ellison and Snoop jarringly profane. And my performance led *New York Daily News* columnist Playthell Benjamin to label me a "sophist" and a "snake oil salesman." (Benjamin would later repeat these, and much stronger claims, when we went head-to-head at hearings on gangsta rap before the Pennsylvania State Legislature and on CBS radio's *Gil Gross Show*.)

Admittedly, much of the resistance I've encountered may have a lot to do with the fact that I'm a wanna-be rap star. I've even been labeled a "hip-hop intellectual." You see, even when I'm lecturing on dense theoretical issues, like, say, the relation of postmodern notions of identity to African-American culture, I've got the grating habit of dropping a line or two—okay, a few stanzas—from the latest rap release. At 37, I came along a little too late to spend my youth spinning tales about my hood in poetic meters padded by James Brown samples. It's probably pretty sad, and often maddening, for folk to see a late baby boomer like me—so late that my generation's been called "'tweeners" because we fit between real baby boomers and Generation Xers—trying to horn in on a younger age group's territory. It's probably a pre-midlife crisis, a forward-looking relapse back into a hip-hop youth that was never really mine. Or maybe in the spirit of hip-hop, I'm simply turning the tables to sample the youth of artists who sample the music of my youth.

Much of the anger I've seen directed at black youth, especially from older blacks, is tied to a belief that young blacks are very different from any other black generation. Among esteemed black intellectuals and persons on the street, there is a consensus that something has gone terribly wrong with black youth. They are disrespectful to their elders. They are obsessed with sex. They are materialistic. They are pathological. They are violent. They are nihilistic. They are ethically depraved. They are lazy. They are menaces to society.

Right away we must admit that some of these complaints form the rhetorical divide that grows between all generations. Some of these cants and carps are no more than predecessor blues. They are the laments of those who come Before judging those who come After. (Such judgments travel a two-way street. Our kids have their share of disgust about the world they've inherited.)

But many of these complaints reflect a real fear of black youth that's not confined to black communities and not explained by any "generation gap." It's hard to open a newspaper or watch television without getting an ugly reminder of the havoc our kids wreak on the streets and the terror they must confront without much sympathy or support. To be sure, the media has irresponsibly painted many of the problems of urban America black or brown. In reality, a lot of our social misery, including drugs, crime, and violence, has a decidedly whiter hue. Still, black youth are in big trouble.

For many black and white Americans, hip-hop culture crudely symbolizes the problems of urban black youth. The list of offenses associated with hip-hop culture is culled from rap lyrics and the lifestyles they promote. The list includes vulgar language, sexism, misogyny, homophobia, sexual promiscuity, domestic abuse, parental disrespect, rejection of authority, and the glorification of violence, drug use, rape, and murder. And it's true that even a casual listen to a lot of hip-hop will turn up these and other nefarious attitudes. At least if you listen to the style of hip-hop known as gangsta rap. The gangsta rap genre of hip-hop emerged in the late '80s on the West Coast as crack and gangs ruled the urban centers of Los Angeles, Long Beach, Compton, and Oakland. Since hip-hop has long turned to the black ghetto and the Latino barrio for lyrical inspiration, it was inevitable that a form of music that mimicked the violence on the streets would rise.

It was just as predictable, though not to the degree that it has happened, that a huge backlash against gangsta rap and black youth would emerge. Among the factors that made black youth culture ripe for such an attack is a general ignorance about the range and depth of hip-hop culture. Ironically, this ignorance helped make gangsta rap an economically viable music. Anti-rap crusader C. Delores Tucker can shout as loud as she wants, and she's certainly earned the right, but she was nowhere to be found when rap group Public Enemy was at its revolutionary height calling for a united black nation to fight racism and the powers that be. True, their brand of hip-hop brushed too closely to anti-Semitism and they certainly could have used a few lessons in feminist thought. But few people quit listening to Sinatra's "Fly Me to the Moon" (it was really named "In Other Words," but Sinatra's Billie Holiday–inspired phrasing was so impeccably memorable that he shifted the song's emphasis) because of his occasional racism or his denigration of women as broads.

The moral of the story is that had more support been given to so-called positive hip-hoppers and to revolutionary rappers who detested body bags and beer bottles; who encouraged black men to "be a father to your child"; who advocated love and respect for black women; who sought to build black communities; and who encouraged youth to study black history, the gangsta rap tide might have been stemmed. At the least, gangsta rappers might have been forced to take the internal criticisms of their hip-hop peers more seriously because such criticisms would have had moral and economic support. After all, it's easier to get an album made if you're "pimpin' hoes," "cockin' glocks," or generally bitch-baiting your way through yet another tired tale about how terrible it was to come up in the hood without your father while blaming your mama for the sorry job she did, than if you're promoting radical black unity or the overthrow of white racism.

This is not to dis West Coast rap. They got big the old-fashioned way: they earned it. Left in the shadow of East Coast rap for years, West Coast rap reinvigorated the hip-hop game by reinventing the premise of rap: to groove the gluteus maximus. As Ralph Ellison said, geography is fate. West Coast hip-hop tailored its fat bass beats and silky melodies for jeeps that cruise the generous spaces of the

West. The music appeals as well to fans in the open spaces of the Midwest and the South. The tightly drawn grooves and cerebral lyrics of the East Coast have almost become site-specific. East Coast rappers cling to beliefs in their artistic superiority and adhere to the principles of authentic hip-hop. Such beliefs give rise to poetically intense rappers like Nas or the esoteric basement hip-hoppers Wu Tang Clan. For the most part, East Coast rap lags far behind the West Coast in record sales and in popularity. Both brands of hip-hop proved too bruising for the old heads of the black bourgeoisie. The music also escaped the artistic interests of a lot of working-class black parents pulling twelve-hour shifts to keep out of the poorhouse.

But their children surely got the message. And so did the children of white suburbia. The crossover of hip-hop to white teens is certainly a driving force behind the attack on black youth. Hip-hop's appeal to white youth extends the refashioning of mainstream America by black popular culture. From sports to fashion, from music to film, innovations in American art owe a debt to the creativity of black culture. For example, 25 years ago, it was unimaginable that black basketball stars would make television commercials or have sneakers named after them. Teams like the New York Knickerbockers were derisively dubbed the New York "Niggerbockers" because of their share of the black talent beginning to flood the NBA. Today, the NBA is a black man's game. Michael Jordan is the most revered and perhaps the richest athlete in the world. Kids of every color lace up his shoes, sport his jersey, and want to, as the ad goes, "Be like Mike."

White kids are also adopting the dress, diction, and demeanor of urban black youth. From baggy pants to oversize shirts, the "gear" of hip-hop culture has been mass-produced and worn by youth of every ethnic and racial group. The slang of hip-hop is now widely used. "Yo" and "Whassup?" are part of our common cultural parlance. The *Arsenio Hall Show* was an extended hip-hop anthem, a limited scope of themes pegged to samples of existing material that are endlessly remixed. Perhaps that's why Hall's show lasted as long as the average rap career, proving that the genre's virtue is its vice. Even the *New York Times* regularly uses "dis" in its articles. The swagger of black youth, the sultry way they combine boasting and self-confidence, has influenced the styles of upper-middle-class white youth. For many white parents, however, such a trend is cause for concern. While white youth already face their version of the generation gap—they've been dubbed "slackers" and "Generation X"—emulating the styles, speech, and behavior of urban black youth is even more menacing.

Of course, there's nothing new about white kids imitating black kids. Neither is this the first time that white panic has followed white teens' adoration of black stars. When Sam Cooke's mellifluous voice and flawless good looks sent white girls screaming in the '50s, it caused an uproar among white adults. And now that white girls are driven crazy by Snoop Doggy Dogg's canine comeliness, especially when there's no doubt about what he wants to do in his dog pound, rap and the culture that produces it are found wanting. It wasn't until rap made a huge impact on white kids that the music was so roundly attacked. As long as the "bad" effects of rap were restricted to black kids, its menace went undetected, unprotested, or it was flat-out ignored.

Among many black adults, hip-hop culture represents a tragic rejection of the values that prevailed in black communities years ago, at least during their youthful watch on the wall of black progress. To hear legions of black adults tell it, there was a time when a black child could be disciplined by any adult in the neighborhood if he or she did wrong. Such a story is meant to show the strength, unity, and durability of black communities of the past. It is also meant to underscore the weakness, fragmentation, and collapse of black communities today. (Once, when I visited a university to lecture, I heard this same story repeated by a black youth, all of eighteen years old, who included her generation among the duly disciplined children. Most blacks would say that her generation is unfamiliar with such an experience. That gave me a clue that such stories are, in large part, rhetorical devices that transmit folk wisdom from one generation to the next. Such stories help us define the limits of acceptable behavior.)

It's clear that the rise of hip-hop culture has provoked a deep black nostalgia for a time when black communities were quite different than they are now. When children respected their elders. When adults, not young thugs, ruled over neighborhoods. When the moral fabric of black communities was knit together by a regard for law and order. When people shared what they had, even if it was their last crust of bread or drop of soup. When families extended beyond blood or biology to take in young people in need of rearing. When communication between blacks on the street was marked by courtesy more than cursing. When black folk went to church, and even if they didn't, respected the minister as a source of moral authority. And on and on.

There's little doubt that black communities of the past were sharply different than they are now. But black communities weren't the idyllic places that nostalgic black folk make them out to be. Nostalgia is colored memory. It is romantic remembering. It recreates as much as it recalls. The political force of black nostalgia—built on a vision of the black past as a utopian, golden age—is harmful to debates about black youth. Every culture, age, and generation has a high point whose benefits are unsurpassable. Such utopias and golden ages, and the benefits they bestow, are usually realized after the fact. Indeed, they have to be. It takes decline to highlight a pinnacle. But when blacks use nostalgia to make moral distinctions between the sort of people black communities produced Then and produce Now, we unravel the very fabric of racial memory that we claim our youth desperately need.

A cure for such nostalgia can be found in works like *Morals and Manners Among Negro Americans,* edited in 1914 by W.E.B. Du Bois and Augustus Dill. Du Bois and Dill surveyed hundreds of leading blacks about the "manners and morals" of black youth. Wouldn't you know it? Many black leaders lamented the negative impact of popular culture on black youth. One leader blamed moral decline on movies, which "have an unwholesome effect upon the young people. Roller skating, ragtime music, cabaret songs, and ugly suggestions of the big city are all pernicious. The dancing clubs in the big cities are also vicious." Another leader worried that black youth "hang around the corners in great numbers, especially the boys. Many of them are becoming gamblers and idlers." Keep in mind that these degenerate black youth make up a generation now praised for its high morals. That should stop us from writing the epitaph of what has been mislabeled a lost generation of black youth. (Even here, racial distinctions prevail. If white kids are demonized as "slackers," at least they're seen to be slacking off from a Protestant work ethic they can recover through hard work. What can you do when you're lost? Often, you get written off. That happens to too many black youth.)

The relation of nostalgic blacks to hip-hop culture can be viewed in the following way: there is a perception of *aesthetic alienation* and *moral strangeness* in black youth. Both of these perceptions, I believe, depend on a denial of crucial aspects of history and racial memory. Amnesia and anger have teamed up to rob many blacks of a balanced perspective on our kids. With such balance, we might justly criticize and appreciate hip-hop culture. Without the moderating influence of historical insight, joined to what might be called the humility of memory, we end up mirroring the outright repudiation our kids face across this country.

SINCE SO MUCH OF THE POLITICS OF NOSTALGIA are about how things used to be, we've got to understand a bit better how things actually were. Now, I don't harbor any illusions about being able, as we used to say in my black ghetto neighborhood in Detroit, to get to "wie es eigentlich gewesen," or, "how it really was." (Me and my boys repeated that line from nineteenth-century historian Leopold von Ranke when we were frustrated in our quest for eighteenth-century philosopher Immanuel Kant's "ding an sich," or, "the thing in itself." Yeah, we had it like that back in the day. No wonder my generation wants our kids to be just like us!) But we must escape the awkward burden of remembering only what we choose to believe by getting a more insightful account of things as they happened. The past should be a fountain of wisdom and warning. It is inevitable that fictions attach to what used to be. But it is immoral to make those fictions the ground of harsh judgments of our children.

The aesthetic alienation of hip-hop has partly to do with perception. Rap is seen as wildly differing from the styles, themes, and tones of previous black music. Well, that's true and not true. Certainly the form of hip-hop is distinct. The skeletal rap crew is composed of a DJ (disc jockey), a producer, and an MC (master of ceremonies, or rapper). (Technology has enhanced, occasionally blurred, and sometimes redivided the crew's labor over the last fifteen years.) In many cases, there are at least a couple of rappers. In some cases, there are several. The DJ commands a pair of phonograph turntables. Among other functions, the DJ plays fragments of records through a technique called scratching: manually rotating a record in sharp, brief bursts of back and forth rhythmic movement over isolated portions of a song, producing a scratching sound.

The producer has several devices at her command, including a beat box and a digital sampler. The beat box, or drum machine, is an electronic instrument that simulates the sound of a drum set. A digital sampler is a synthesizer that stores in its computerized memory a variety of sounds (a James Brown scream, a TV theme song, a guitar riff, a bass line) that are reproduced when activated by the producer. The DJ and the producer work together in laying down backing tracks for the MC. The tracks consist of rhythms, scratches, beats, shrieks, noise, other sound effects, and loops, which are fragments of existing songs reworked and repeated in new musical contexts.

The MC, or rapper, recites lyrics in a rhythmic, syncopated fashion. The rapper's rhetorical quirks, vocal tics, rhyme flow, and verbal flourishes mark his or her individual style. In the early days of rap, MCs often simulated sonic fragments with their voices, causing some rappers to be dubbed human beat boxes. Rappers can use a variety of rhyme schemes, from couplets in tetrameter to iambic pentameter. Their rhyme schemes can employ masculine and feminine rhymes, assonantal and consonantal rhymes, or even internal rhymes. Rappers may use enjambment, prosody, and sophisticated syncopations to tie their collage of rhymes into a pleasing sonic ensemble.

But hip-hop's form joins features of black oral culture, especially toasts (long narrative poems) and the dozens, to a variety of black musical styles. As Gil Scott-Heron once remarked, hip-hop fuses the drum and the word. Blues music is the style of black artistry most closely associated with hip-hop. The blues spawned stock characters within its lyrical universe, including the hoochie-coochie man, the mojo worker, the lover man, and the bad man bluesman. Their relation to hip-hop's (and '70s blaxploitation flicks') macks, pimps, hustlers, and gangsters is clear. Plus, the rhetorical marks and devices of blues culture, including vulgar language, double entendres, boasting, and liberal doses of homespun machismo, link it to hip-hop, especially gangsta rap. And in case you're thinking, "Yeah, but the blues and early jazz weren't nearly as nasty as rap," think again. There are lyrics contained in the songs of the great Jelly Roll Morton, for example, that would make Snoop Doggy Dogg wince in embarrassment. You can read Morton's lyrics in their most distinguished place of storage, the Library of Congress. (Does this mean in the next century that that august institution will house the Dogg's Magnum Snoopus, "Doggystyle" for future generations to lap up or howl at?) Modern technology, together with the urban and secular emphases of black culture, has helped expose localized traditions of vulgar black speech—including agrarian blues, signifying, toasts, and the dozens—to a worldwide audience. And millions of blacks are angry and ashamed.

It's clear, too, that '50s rock and roll, '60s soul music, '70s R&B, '80s new jack swing, and '90s hip-hop soul have touched on themes that rap has addressed, though often in a dramatically different style. Some of the most important black music of the '60s and '70s, for instance, attempted to reconcile the political demands of a new black consciousness with the changing rules of domestic life. This music attempted to join erotic desire to its political ambitions. Thus, Marvin Gaye followed his 1971 masterpiece "What's Going On" with his brilliant 1973 release "Let's Get It On," moving from the social to the sexual sphere in exploring the complex dimensions of black culture. While hip-hop addresses these same concerns, its ideological orientation, and therefore its artistic direction, is almost reversed. With the increasing attacks on the black family as an unreliable space to shape sexuality in socially acceptable forms, a lot of hip-hoppers try to join politics to erotic desire. Many artists move from the sexual center of rap to the varieties of political consciousness hip-hop manages to embrace along its cutting edges.

Still, there's no doubt that older styles of black music have provoked their own controversies. But depending on which black generation you speak with, each style represents the golden age of black music. In fact, hip-hoppers themselves have more than a little nostalgia, particularly for '70s culture and music. Their nostalgia is even more ironic, indeed laughable, because of hip-hop's grand claims to authenticity, to "keeping it real." Meaning their music won't sell out by pandering to the styles or themes of R&B. Right. Hip-hop still depends on existing black music even as it reshapes, often brilliantly, the grooves it steals. Without its creative uses of past black music, rap would be a museum of speech with little to inspire us to conserve its words, much less heed its warnings and many lessons.

The technical devices of hip-hop accent its ambiguous relation to history. Through sampling, hip-hop revives and reinvents what has been forgotten. Sampling allows hip-hop to reshape what's been neglected by removing it from the context—the actual album, the network of cultural nuances, the time period—in which it originally came to life. What hip-hop gives with one hand, it takes back with the other. While they make fresh use of a Parliament-Funkadelic beat or a Leon Haywood loop, hip-hoppers often have little awareness of the musical traditions those artists fed on. Such awareness might make rappers' creative piracy much more compelling. How? The rhetoric of rap could rework, satirize, or play off of the intellectual visions of some of the songs it lifts. What rap does so brilliantly with form it might be able to match with content.

Paying more attention to black music's intellectual traditions might keep hip-hop from completely turning its machinery of mythology on itself. Hip-hoppers get misty-eyed about the "old-school" and what happened "back in the day." There is already growing up around rap a wall of myth that excludes crucial features of hip-hop's own history. For instance, its devotees largely contend that hip-hop originated in the black (including West Indian) and Latino working-class ghetto of the South Bronx with block parties in the early '70s. But others have recently argued that hip-hop was born in the West Bronx. More significantly, hip-hop cannot be divorced from its roots in Jamaica. In the 1960s, sound system operators hauled massive speakers in wooden carts in working-class communities during back-yard dances attended by "rude boys," the Caribbean counterpart to hip-hop's "b-boys." Also, the Jamaican dance hall was the site of a mixture of older and newer forms of Caribbean music, including calypso, soca, salsa, Afro-Cuban, ska, and reggae. One of the first great pioneers of hip-hop, DJ Kool Herc, was a West Indian immigrant to the West Bronx who brought with him a hunger to recreate the memories and mood of Jamaican dance hall music. Those roots nourish rap.

Hip-hoppers often forget that hip-hop was initially patronized by average working-class and middle-class kids, not gangsters or other members of the hard-core scene. Afrika Bambaataa, another old-school pioneer who created hip-hop standards like "Looking for the Perfect Beat" and "Planet Rock," also founded the Universal Zulu Nation. True enough, the organization grew out of South Bronx gang life (Bambaataa was a member of the notorious gang Black Spades). But Universal Zulu Nation was committed to peace, unity, and self-knowledge. And neither was hip-hop an exclusively black affair. African-Americans, Afro-Caribbeans, Latinos, and progressive whites all shared in the Bronx parties where hip-hop was spawned in the States. Hip-hop's multiethnic audience helped energize its free-form expression. Old-school legends like DJ Grandmaster Flash experimented with a wide range of music, from Frank Sinatra to Thin Lizzy.

It may not be altogether unfitting that hip-hop is partially cut off from the roots of even its own history. After all, with its impulse to create sonic collages, its sampling of existing music, its disregard for musical conventions, and its irreverent pairing of the culturally sacred and profane, hip-hop is thought to be a striking instance of postmodernism. And according to critic Fredric Jameson, the lack of a sense of history rests squarely at the center, if it can be said to have one, of the postmodern moment. While it's easy to see why hip-hop is deemed a postmodern art form—quotation, pastiche, contingency, fragmentation and the like help define its presence—it may be that its homegrown nostalgia and hunger for purity and authenticity betray modernist obsessions.

In other words, the postmodernism of hip-hop may show that we're trying to get rid of, or, at least, get over modernism too quickly. Postmodernism may turn out to be modernism in drag. At its heart, modernism looks back to move forward. Modernism is obsessed with critically reexamining the ground of its origin—which, in its advocates' minds, turns out to be our culture's origins—so that its foundations are secured. Modernist discussions are caught up in the rapture of renewal, recovery, return, and renaissance, all in the name of progress, of moving forward. The new is valuable precisely because it is formed out of reappropriating the original. The great paradox of modernism, for some critics, is that, in order to outdo it, one must hold that whatever will succeed modernism, say postmodernism, is rooted in a ground of thought that is more original than the modernist ground it criticizes. Ironically, that's a modernist move. As a result, one ends up replacing the content of modernism, but not the form of modernism itself. That's why critic Theodor Adorno said that there was no overcoming modernity.

The question of whether hip-hop is really postmodernist or modernist is, at some levels, a strictly academic affair. In other ways, the debate may help us understand the conflicts, and the hidden ties, between hip-hop and forms of black music that have modernist elements. It may shed light on the uses black folk make of their past, and the difference those uses make in how we view black youth.

IF BLACK NOSTALGIA HAS DISTORTED the relation of postmodern black youth culture to a complex black past, this is nowhere more powerfully glimpsed than in comparing hip-hop with a high point of black modernism: jazz music and culture. Critics like Stanley Crouch and musicians like Wynton Marsalis have relentlessly attacked hip-hop culture for its deficits when compared to jazz. In conversations—in truth, they were herculean arguments between us that raged for hours at a time—neither of these gifted gentlemen has had anything good to say about hip-hop culture.

Crouch maintains that hip-hop is, in a memorable phrase comparing rap to the infamous, racist 1915 D.W. Griffith film, "*Birth of a Nation* with a backbeat." Marsalis thinks rap reflects a fascism that mars humane art. Plus, rap is rooted in a banal, mindless repetition of beat, signaling a lack of musical imagination and invention. Inspired by the likes of Ralph Ellison, but especially by Albert Murray, Crouch and Marsalis argue that the artistic possibilities of jazz—its heart pumping with the blood of improvisation, its gut churning with the blues—embody the edifying quest for romantic self-expression and democratic collaboration that capture Negro music and American democracy at their best. For Crouch and Marsalis, hip-hop negates everything jazz affirms.

Many fans of black music, including stalwarts of soul and R&B, most certainly agree. They simply add their music of preference, and perhaps their own string of modifiers, to Crouch and Marsalis's list. (That's because Aretha ain't about democracy. She's about the imperious demands of gospel genius as it baptizes and is transformed by secular sentiments. I'm not so sure that Crouch and Marsalis stand ready, however, to reciprocate. Whether Aretha, Sam Cooke, Otis Redding, Marvin Gaye, Donny Hathaway, or Al Green counts in their reckoning as much as, say, early Miles or middle Coltrane, Sarah Vaughan or Ella Fitzgerald, or Ellington or Armstrong, is highly doubtful.) Despite the issues that separate black musical purists of any sort, their shared disdain for hip-hop culture's claims to art unite them as citizens of the Republic of Nostalgia.

The only problem is that, like hip-hop, jazz has a history of cultural attack. That history has been buried under an avalanche of nostalgia that hides jazz's grittier roots. For instance, during the Jazz Age and the Harlem Renaissance, the response to jazz by a large segment of the black bourgeoisie, black intellectuals, and black artists anticipated the attack on rap. Such responses reflected, and were partly driven by, the negative response to jazz of large segments of white society. Jazz was viewed as a cultural and artistic form that compromised decency and morality. It was linked to licentious behavior and lewd artistic gestures. With its "jungle rhythms," its blues base, its double entendre lyrics, and its sexually aggressive dancing, jazz, like hip-hop today, was the most widely reviled music of the 1920s and '30s. Headlines in respectable publications asked questions like: "Did Jazz Put the Sin in Syncopation?". According to the *Ladies Home Journal,* jazz was responsible for a "holocaust" of illegitimate births. A Cincinnati-based Catholic newspaper railed against the "sensuous" music of jazz. It said that "the embracing of partners—the female only half dressed—is absolutely indecent." Blues pioneer W.C. Handy's daughter, Lucille, was sternly admonished by the Colored Girls' Circle of an elite school for "making a fool" of herself by singing and dancing her father's blues and jazz. "It [continuing to sing and dance] will be under the peril of death and great danger to yourself," the letter concluded.

Many Harlem Renaissance intellectuals detested "gin, jazz, and sex." The publications of black organizations, from the NAACP's magazine, *Crisis,* edited by W.E.B. Du Bois, to the Socialist Party–supported magazine, *Messenger,* edited by A. Philip Randolph and Chandler Owens (with assistance from George Schuyler), expressed opposition to jazz as well. For many Harlem Renaissance intellectuals, jazz was not viewed as a serious artistic achievement on par with European classical music. The great irony of blacks worshiping European music is that European composers such as Richard Strauss were, at the same time, expressing profound admiration for jazz.

In 1926, one of the most important debates about the relation of black intellectuals to black mass culture took place in the pages of the *Nation,* between George Schuyler and Langston Hughes. In his essay, "The Negro Art Hokum," Schuyler argued that there was no such thing as a distinct Negro art apart from American art. Schuyler said that Negro art occurred in Africa, but to "suggest the possibility of any such development among the ten million colored people in this republic is self-evident foolishness." Schuyler argued that "slave songs based on Protestant hymns and biblical texts" and "secular songs of sorrow and tough luck known as the blues" were "contributions of a caste" in certain sections of America that were "foreign to Northern Negroes, West Indian Negroes, and African Negroes." For Schuyler, defining art in racial terms was "hokum."

Hughes's response, which ran a week later, became one of his signature essays. Entitled "The Negro Artist and the Racial Mountain," Hughes's essay lamented the veiled desire of some black artists to be white. Such artists feared their own racial identity. Hughes argued that the black middle class was denying a crucial part of its heritage by denying the "beauty of [its] own people" and that Negroes should stop imitating "Nordic manners, Nordic faces, Nordic air, Nordic art." In their stead, he urged Negroes to embrace "the low-down folks, the so-called common element, and they are the majority—may the Lord be praised." Hughes argued that the "common people will give to the world its truly great Negro artist, the one who is not afraid to be himself."

For Hughes, the racial mountain was the inability of the black bourgeoisie to accept Negro art from the masses. Hughes exhorted his fellow Negroes to let "the blare of Negro jazz bands and the bellowing voice of Bessie Smith singing blues penetrate the closed ears of the colored near-intellectuals until they listen and perhaps understand." Hughes's words are still relevant.

By rehearsing this bit of jazz history—one that is conveniently overlooked by Crouch and Marsalis as they attack rap and proclaim jazz as America's classical music—I am not arguing that we should romanticize black folk culture. Neither am I equating black folk art and pop culture. The big business of how black culture is packaged as a commodity to be bought and sold in the marketplace with billions of dollars at stake prevents such an easy equation. I'm simply arguing that all forms of black music have been attacked both within and beyond black culture. Blues and jazz, rhythm and blues, and soul have all been viewed as indecent, immoral, and corrupting of black youth. To be nostalgic for a time when black music offered a purer aesthetic or a higher moral vision is to hunger for a time in history that simply doesn't exist. (Of course, another way of stating this is to say that all black music has an aesthetic appeal, and a moral vision, that will at first be assailed, but whose loss will one day be mourned and compared favorably with the next form of hated black music to come along.) When Marsalis, Crouch, and other critics perched aloft the wall of high black culture throw stones at hip-hop, they forget that such stones were once thrown at their music of preference. Bebop was once hip-hop. Ragtime was once rap. Bluesmen were once b-boys. What is now noble was once notorious.

I'm not suggesting that there are no artistic differences between generations and styles of black music. Queen of

Hip-hop Soul Mary J. Blige is no Queen of Soul Aretha Franklin. (With Aretha's gifts, very few have measured up. Those who do—such figures as Vanessa Bell Armstrong, Ann Nesby, and the late Marion Williams—flourish in the gospel realm.) And neither should she be. She couldn't be even if she wanted to. Aretha's art, in large part, draws from her sheer genius. The outsized technical ambitions encouraged in her by the gospel tradition of the black church. Her apprenticeship in sanctified emotion under gospel great Clara Ward and her famous preacher father, C.L. Franklin. And a voice whose only teachers were unrelenting pathos and undaunted passion. But Aretha's greatest art has to do with a budding black feminist consciousness in the '60s and '70s. The demand for respect. The warning to men to think about their emotional intents with women. The prescription of feel-good therapies for sexual intimacy. And reckoning with the endless chain of fools produced by the quest for faithful love. In short, Aretha Franklin's greatness is a product of its times.

Mary J. Blige's art is similarly a product of its times. True enough, hip-hop soul borrows the grooves, and the rhetorical gravity, of black soul culture. But hip-hop soul's themes and rhythms occupy a distinct spiritual orbit. Blige says much of what Aretha said in the '60s and '70s, but she says it in the grittier, more explicit voice of hip-hop culture. Blige's hip-hop soul feminism seeks real love. But it remakes edifying love confessions into gut-wrenching pleas of faithfulness. It makes self-love the basis of loving others. And it bitterly, defiantly refuses to accept sexual infidelity (though Aretha hinted as much when she said if men wanted do-right women they'd have to be do-right men). Blige is full of self-enclosed hip-hop angst. She also possesses, or at least she seeks to possess, a strong degree of hip-hop self-reliance. And she has a dark, stormy, rap-inflected (or is that infected?) artistic temperament.

Blige's art reshapes the blues at the bottom of Aretha's soul feminism into a brooding female voice of resistance in an Age of Misogyny. Aretha's generation certainly faced the same forces. But '60s and '70s sexism was cloaked beneath a chivalry and condescension that even black male versions of patriarchy could express. (Let's not forget that there were plenty of brutal examples of black men mistreating black women at Aretha's artistic peak. Lyrically speaking, male rappers talk a good game of ho-smacking and bitch-beating, but the likes of James Brown, Bill Withers, David Ruffin, Marvin Gaye, and a host of other artists allegedly abused wives, girlfriends, or lovers while singing sweet, rapturous praises to the fairer sex on wax.) Aretha Franklin's and Mary J. Blige's aesthetic values reflect, in part, the cultural and musical environments that shape their art. What they respond to—norms, practices, behaviors, expectations, ideas—has as great an effect on the character of their art as their particular musical gifts. While soul and hip-hop cultures embody virtues to which each musical style responds, the cultures contain vices to which each style reacts. (Franklin and Blige, of course, embody both the good and the bad of their respective traditions in their art.) The explicitness of hip-hoppers makes their limitations more obvious. But the subtlety of soul artists doesn't make their limitations any less lethal.

THE PROBLEM WITH NOSTALGIC BLACKS is that they place more artistic stock in the aesthetic form they are familiar with. (They often have what may be termed Hegel's problem, named after the philosopher who believed that of all periods in history, the Zeitgeist, the world spirit, was best embodied in his own Prussian state during his life. For our nostalgic true believers, it translates into the notion that the best in black music happened to coincide with their own youth.) At the same time, they associate vice, or limitation, or smallness of artistic vision, with the aesthetic form most alien to them. While blues, jazz, soul, and R&B may share crucial assumptions, say, about women, the differences in their outward aesthetic forms makes us believe that one is more harmful or more foreign to black culture than the other. Thus, hip-hop's misogyny is more jolting than the antipathy toward women that came through in some R&B. But within both hip-hop and what's called urban contemporary music, there are artists who are appalled at the malevolence hurled at black women. And one need not look beyond these genres to find rich expressions of the seductive art of subtlety—as opposed to the "do me" explicitness common among current acts—practiced by artists of previous generations. Chante Moore and Tony Terry, Maxwell and Babyface, Prince Markie Dee and Heavy D are just a few.

But nostalgia can't explain every negative assessment of black pop culture. Even if it did, it wouldn't mean that all such judgments are necessarily wrong, even if they're made for the wrong reasons. It may be that all the explanations about different artistic ages—and the limitations and possibilities each age presents—simply can't change the fact that Mary J. Blige isn't Aretha Franklin. Fine. But that's not an indictment of hip-hop soul per se. It's a value judgment about artists exploring similar though distinct genres at different times. I'm simply arguing that we respect the rules of each genre. We should adjust our evaluations of music based on the sorts of achievement that are possible, even desirable, in a given period. That doesn't mean we can't rank them. After all, some music is more complicated than other music. Some art forms take more mastery than others. But we should rank these different styles of music fairly. As important as it is, complexity of achievement is not the only value worth recognizing or celebrating in art. Plus, there are many kinds of artistic complexity that merit our attention.

After all, our age has seen the likes of Whitney Houston, Anita Baker, and Mariah Carey, gifted artists of a greatly changed black sound, whatever that means, whose skills of delivery and interpretation far exceed the schlock that riddles so much contemporary black pop. (Still, each has contributed her fair share of misfires, as is true, of course, of the inimitable Ms. Franklin.) Contemporary hip-hop soul has also brought forth artists like D'Angelo. His young career holds promise for melding the wispy melodies of '70s soul to hip-hop rhythms and occasionally raunchy sensibilities. And male groups Boys II Men and Jodeci, and female groups En Vogue and SWV rise above the mediocrity of their chosen idioms.

But that's just the point. Aretha outdid most of her peers whose names we have long since forgotten. Their failures, or better still, their relative successes, don't invalidate the genres of black music in which they strived to make sublime art. Soul music is judged by its brilliance, not its blight. It is measured by its supreme visions, not its short-sighted trends. Like all great music, it is measured by the size of its aspirations—which are measured by the aspirations of its greatest artists, even the unsung ones—not simply by artists who managed to make the charts or to win the awards. (Donny Hathaway was never justly recognized for his extraordinary genius as a composer, artist, and musician. And Little Willie John was one of the greatest—some argue, *the* greatest—R&B singers, but few people know his name or work, except as it's drained of its pathos by more famous but less gifted white artists.) Hip-hop is no different. It's not the mindless, numbing pornography of the notorious 2 Live Crew that is the measure of hip-hop's vitality, but the rhetorical, lyrical ingenuity of Rakim or Nas. Snoop Doggy Dogg's seductive and highly accomplished rhyme flow, and Ice Cube's narrative powers—plus Dr. Dre's pulsating, harmonically complex G-funk—define gangsta rap's metier. Not the mediocre rants of the late Eazy-E—although his brilliance as impresario and record producer, even talent scout, is undeniable. A lot of hip-hop is okay, more of it is good, and a little of it is great. Just like any other music.

(Crouch, Marsalis, and other critics have argued against hip-hop even being called serious music. Of course, these critics hold the same grudge against latter-day Coltrane, Eric Dolphy, Ornette Coleman, Cecil Taylor, Albert Ayler, Archie Shepp, Don Cherry, and almost any avant-garde jazz artist who championed unorthodox harmonies, departure from chord-based improvisations, atonal "noise," and dissonant melodies. Neither Ellington nor Armstrong, heroes for Crouch and Marsalis—and for me, too—would be today what they were when they played. To be sure, they'd still be geniuses. But the character of their genius would be greatly altered. Their relentless reach for the edge of experience pushed them to keep growing, experimenting, and improvising. Conservative advocates of jazz end up freezing the form, making jazz an endless series of explorations of already charted territory. It's a process of rediscovering what's already been discovered. Such a process led Gary Giddins to remark that the problem with so much of contemporary neotraditionalist jazz is that Thelonius Monk couldn't even win the annual contest that's sponsored in his name! The very spirit of jazz—its imperative to improvise, which can often lead into dangerous, unmapped territory—is thus sacrificed in the name of preserving the noble, heroic traditions that grow out of a specific time in jazz's history. What's really being preserved is the product, not the process, of improvisation. But that's another book.)

At base, the perception of the aesthetic alienation of hip-hop culture is linked to a perception that black youth are moral strangers. I mean by "moral strangers" that black youth are believed to be ethically estranged from the moral practices and spiritual beliefs that have seen previous black generations through harsh and dangerous times. The violence of black youth culture is pointed to as a major symptom of moral strangeness. Heartless black-on-black murder, escalating rates of rape, rising incidents of drug abuse, and the immense popularity of hip-hop culture reinforce the perception of an ethical estrangement among black youth. In arguing the moral strangeness of black youth, many critics recycle bits and pieces of old-style arguments about the pathology of black urban culture. Widely popularized in Daniel Moynihan's famous 1965 study of the black family—whose pathology was partially ascribed to a growing matriarchy in black domestic life—the notion that black culture carries the seeds of its own destruction is an old idea. The argument for black cultural pathology is really an updated version of beliefs about black moral deficiency as ancient as the black presence in the New World.

More recently, Cornel West has attempted to explain the problems of black culture by pointing to its nihilism. Since the nihilism argument has been used by many critics to prove the moral strangeness of black youth, I'll explore it in some detail before arguing for an alternate perspective.

For West, nihilism is "the profound sense of psychological depression, personal worthlessness, and social despair so widespread in black America." West wants to unblinkingly stare down the problems of black culture, and to call a spade a spade: black crime is increasing, suicide is rising, hopelessness is spreading, and ethical surrender is pandemic. Yet liberals, West argues, simply close their eyes or believe that if they say what they see they'll be thought of as cold conservatives. West also knows that mere moral corrosion, as argued by conservatives, is not large enough an explanation for what's going on in black culture. West seeks to avoid the pitfalls of both conservative behaviorists and liberal structuralists by arguing for a complex vision of black culture that takes into account the "saturation of market forces and market moralities" in black life, while highlighting the crisis of black leadership. For West, such a strategy allows us to be frank in our discussions of black moral and spiritual collapse while refusing to scapegoat those blacks who are victimized by dehumanizing forces.

West is right to grapple with issues of morality and behavior, matters that are largely taboo for the left. He's also right to zoom in on the market forces and market moralities that besiege black culture. Still, as an explanation for what ails us, nihilism has severe problems. First, nihilism is seen as a cause, not a consequence, of black suffering. The collapse of hope, the spiritual despair that floods black America, the clinical depression we suffer, are all the pernicious result of something more basic than black nihilism: white racism. (The list includes economic suffering, class inequality, and material hardship as well, but I'll get to those in a bit.) I don't mean here just the nasty things many white folk believe about black folk. I'm referring to the systematic destruction of black life, the pervasive attack on the black sense of well-being, the subversion of black self-determination, and the erasure of crucial narratives of black self-esteem that are foundational to American versions of democracy. Nihilism is certainly self-destructive. That's because black folk were taught—and have had it reinforced across time, geography, and ideology—that our black selves weren't worth loving or preserving. Nihilism is the outgrowth, not the origin, of such harsh lessons. Without the destruction of white supremacy, black nihilism will continue to grow.

Then too, nihilism shifts the burden for getting black America back on track to suffering black folk. That seems an awful tall order for a people already strapped with sparse resources and weighted down with nihilism. West argues for a politics of conversion, where a love ethic is central. As a Baptist preacher and former pastor, I am deeply sympathetic to this. The logic of such a duty, however, might be questioned. Love without resources will not ultimately solve the problems black folk face. With enough resources—employment, education, housing, food—black folk will have the luxury, the leisure, the reasonable chance to love themselves. Of course, I'm not suggesting that poor black folk without such resources don't or can't love themselves. But I am suggesting that love alone, even a complex, socially rooted understanding of love, cannot provide the material basis for the permanent high self-regard that will need to be in place for black folk to stop snuffing one another out. The presence of such resources cannot by themselves guarantee a good outcome. But we can be reasonably assured that, without such resources, a bad outcome is highly likely.

Plus, if black nihilism is really that pervasive, can nihilists resolve nihilism? Can folk for whom hope has been eclipsed really muster the moral might to throw off the psychic chains of their suffering? Conversion—which leads me to believe that this is in part a project of self-help—is a necessary, but insufficient, basis to turn back the nihilistic tide. While Martin Luther King wanted to convert white racists, he also wanted to put in place a structure of laws, duties, and obligations that had the power to change behavior. Given the choice of love and power, King took power, and let the love come later. (King said, for instance, that the law may not make whites love blacks, but it could stop them from lynching blacks. Of course, it is a dialectical process: love insists on the right laws, and the right sort of laws provide a framework for—one hopes—the eventual development of love, which could, in turn, obviate the laws. These poles are united in King's beliefs.) True enough, King's life and ministry were regulated by a love ethic. But he saw righteous power, that is, power linked to justice, as the imperfect but indispensable social translation of love.

Finally, West's theory of nihilism is driven by a nostalgic vision of black life. West says that "the genius of our black foremothers and forefathers was to create powerful buffers to ward off the nihilistic threat." West also argues that our foreparents were equipped with "cultural armor to beat back the demons of hopelessness, meaninglessness, and lovelessness." The armor included "values of service and sacrifice, love and care, discipline and excellence." Black religious and civic institutions helped black folk survive.

West is certainly right that black folk kept on keeping on, that they refused to give up. But for my money, those things haven't gone away. It's too early to tell if black folk have surrendered the fight. But I guess I just don't see where nihilism is winning, where the attempts of black folk to make a way out of no way have ceased. The black church continues to thrive against tremendous odds. Black families continue to strive to make a lie out of the vicious rumors of their inherent pathology. Poor black folk—well, it's a wonder that more haven't given up, surrendered to a life of crime and moral mischief.

The real miracle of contemporary black life is that there are still so many sane, sensible, struggling, secular, sanctified, spiritual, and spunky black folk who just said no to destruction way before Nancy Reagan figured out what crack was. In other words, those black folk of the past are us black folk of the present. Our black youth are not a different moral species than the black youth of the past. They are not moral strangers. And as the quote from Du Bois and Dill above proves, black folk are always worried about their kids. We always romanticize our past, partly as a way to jump-start our flagging efforts in the present. That's certainly okay. It's when nostalgia is used to browbeat and thrust a finger in the face of black youth in an effort to convince them that their moral makeups are grievously defective that nostalgia becomes destructive.

In the end, it may be that the concept of nihilism is symptomatic of the disease it aims to highlight. It may be that a belief in nihilism is too hopeless about the black future, too out of touch with the irreverent spirit of resistance that washes over black culture. A belief in nihilism is too, well, nihilistic. But nostalgia can do that. By viewing the black past as morally and spiritually distinct from the present, we lose sight of the resources for ethical engagement that are carried forward from the past into our own thinking, believing, hoping, praying, and doing. It would be good to remember black preacher and theologian Howard Thurman's wise words, from his book of sermons, *The Growing Edge:*

> At the time when the slaves in America were without any excuse for hope and they could see nothing before them but the long interminable cotton rows and the fierce sun

and the lash of the overseer, what did they do? They declared that God was not through. They said, "We cannot be prisoners of this event. We must not scale down the horizon of our hopes and our dreams and our yearnings to the level of the event of our lives." So they lived through their tragic moment until at last they came out on the other side, saluting the fulfillment of their hopes and their faith, which had never been imprisoned by the event itself.

A belief in nihilism may make us prisoners of present events. A belief in the indomitable spirit of hope that thrives even when things are at their darkest for black folk may be the real link to a powerful black past.

STILL, THERE'S NO DOUBT THAT TERRIBLE THINGS are happening to black youth. To pretend otherwise is to ignore the obvious. Black youth are killing and being killed. Crime and violence go hand in hand. High unemployment is entrenched. Teenage pregnancy is epidemic. How can we explain these facts? I think we've got to move from a theory of moral strangeness to a theory of how power has shifted away from adults to young people in many urban homes and communities. Highlighting such a shift by no means sidesteps issues of morality, values, or responsibility. It simply gives us a handle on specific changes in black youth culture that have had a vicious effect on black life.

I think there is a *juvenocracy* operating in many urban homes and communities. For me, a juvenocracy is the domination of black and Latino domestic and urban life by mostly male figures under the age of 25 who wield considerable economic, social, and moral influence. A juvenocracy may consist of drug gangs, street crews, loosely organized groups, and individual youths who engage in illicit activity.

They operate outside the bounds of the moral and political economies of traditional homes and neighborhoods. The rise of a juvenocracy represents a significant departure from home and neighborhood relations where adults are in charge. Three factors are at the heart of such a shift.

The first is the extraordinary violence of American life. As historian Richard Slotkin has argued, the frontier myth at the base of our country revolves around "regeneration through violence." America renews itself at the altar of devotion to violence as a rite of national identification. It is important to remember this rite as cries go up about the exceptional violence of black youth. Such violence, sadly, is quite mainstream. The prominence of hip-hop culture has provoked fresh attacks on black youth. Black youth are viewed as innately inclined to violent behavior. The lyrics and images of hip-hop are used as proof of such a claim. Well, as strong and pungent as hip-hop is, as offensive as it can be, it is still art. It isn't life, no matter what some hip-hoppers claim about its "realness." Indeed, without making too strong a point of it, hip-hop's existence may be keeping a lot of black youth away from drugs, crime, and life on the streets because they get to rap about such things in the sound booth. Thank God for what other hip-hoppers derisively refer to as "studio gangstas."

It is simply dishonest to paint black youth as the primary source of violence in America. In fact, more often than not, black youth are the victims, not the perpetrators, of violence. Although they are only 5.9 percent of the population, black males account for 40 percent of homicide victims. Black men over 24 are the victims of homicide at a rate of 65.7 per 100,000. For white males in that age group, the figure is 7.8 per 100,000. Youth between the ages of 12 and 17 are the most common victims of crime in America:

1 in 3 stands a chance of being raped, robbed, or mugged. Black youth violence, especially as it is concentrated within a juvenocracy, reflects the violence directed at young black bodies.

Juvenocracies are, in part, mechanisms of defense that develop a vicious life and logic of their own. As most Americans know, it is easy to become addicted to violence. After all, the major broadcast networks average five acts of violence per hour in prime-time. On Saturday mornings, networks average 25 acts of violence an hour. By the time kids reach elementary school, they've seen 100,000 acts of simulated violence. For poor, black children, who watch more television than most, the number is even higher. By the time kids turn eighteen, they've seen almost 18,000 acts of simulated murder on television. Add to that the profusion of gangsta rap narratives and the picture is indeed disturbing.

Since black youth are disproportionately targeted for violence, especially in their own homes, neighborhoods, and schools, the rise of a juvenocracy was predictable. Black youth hang together—in gangs, crews, groups, and so on—for affection and protection. And, yes, for destruction as well. In fact, such behavior does not show an ethical estrangement from American society, but a feverish embrace of its pragmatic principles of survival. Black youth show a frightening moral intimacy with the traditions of American violence. Appealing to a distinction that moral philosophers have made for centuries, the behavior of juvenocrats may not be *reasonable*—its effect on communities, homes, and schools is unreasonably destructive—but in light of the violence and poverty black youth face, the behavior of juvenocrats is certainly *rational.*

The second factor explaining the rise of a juvenocracy is the emergence of what Mike Davis has called the "political economy of crack" in the mid-'80s until the early '90s, which shifted power to young black and Latino males in the homes and on the streets of cities ranging from Los Angeles to Chicago. The manufacturing, packaging, merchandising, and distribution of crack cocaine brought millions of dollars into the hands of formerly impoverished, grossly undereducated black and Latino youth. The postindustrial collapse of many urban areas—brought on by shifts from manufacturing to service industries (over the last twenty years, the U.S. economy lost five million jobs in the manufacturing sector); the decreased production of goods leading to corporate downsizing; technological change; capital flight; and the relocation of corporations to low-wage havens in bordering countries—punched a gaping hole in the legitimate economy for black youth who were already at its margins. The political economy of crack, and the goods and services it allowed black and Latino youth to provide for themselves and their families, helped shift power to young black and Latino males who became de facto heads of households and neighborhood guardians. And menaces. The number of homicides associated with the crack business soared in cities like New York, Los Angeles, and Chicago.

Finally, the rise of the culture of the gun in America drove the emergence of a juvenocracy. The American fetish for loaded weapons of destruction is numbing. In this case, statistics really do tell the story. In 1990, for instance, there were 11,730 people killed by handguns in the United States. In the UK, the figure was 22. In the US there are 201 million firearms in the hands of private citizens; 67 million of these are handguns. Every day, 65 Americans are killed by handgun fire. There are 1 million automatic or semiautomatic weapons circulating in our nation. Thus, it is 20 times more likely that a semiautomatic weapon will be used in a crime in our country than a conventional firearm. Over 1 billion dollars is spent annually for treatment of firearm injuries.

There were 33,651 Americans killed in the Korean War. There were 47,364 Americans killed in the Vietnam War. There were 37,155 Americans killed with firearms in homicides, suicides, and accidents in 1990. In 1991, 45,536 Americans were killed in motor vehicle accidents. The same year, 38,317 Americans died from gunshot wounds. Now firearm incidents surpass motor vehicle accidents as the most likely way Americans will die. Among white Americans, 28.4 per 100,000 die from motor vehicle injuries; 15.2 per 100,000 die from firearms. For Latinos, 28.7 per 100,000 die from motor vehicle accidents; 29.6 per 100,000 die from firearms. For blacks, 23.0 per 100,000 die from motor vehicles; 70.7 per 100,000 die from firearms. In 1990, 12.9 out of 100,000 white males between 20 and 24 were killed by firearms; 140.7 out of 100,000 black males between 20 and 24 were killed by firearms in the same year. One in 28 black males born in the United States is likely to be murdered; 93 percent of black murder victims are killed by other blacks. Firearms in the hands of young black and Latino men has clearly altered the urban landscape. Firearms have given juvenocrats the ultimate weapon of death.

The American addiction to violence, the political economy of crack, and this nation's fetish for firearms account for the rise of a violent juvenocracy. Of course, there are ethical dimensions to juvenocracies as well. Are juvenocracies corrupt? Yes. Are the people who participate in juvenocracies often morally vicious? Yes. Should the destruction that juvenocracies leave in their wake, especially in black and Latino communities, be opposed? With all our might. But unlike culture of pathology arguments, or even arguments about black nihilism, my theory of juvenocracy doesn't locate the source of ethical erosion and moral corruption at the heart of black communities. Why? Because the behavior of juvenocrats can be explained by generic, or better, universal principles of human action. Murder, robbery, assault and battery, and drug dealing are not peculiar to black culture. They occur everywhere. A theory of black pathology or nihilism confuses the matter by asking us to believe that these problems are endemic to black communities. They are not.

A theory of universal human action argues that criminal behavior, and the moral corruption it implies, occur in Italian communities, too, and Korean ones. Should we have theories of Italian pathology, of Korean nihilism? Given that every ethnic and racial group has its unfair share of trouble, it makes no sense to describe such behavior with ethnic or racial modifiers. Of course, crime, pathology, and corruption come in specific shapes. It makes sense to speak openly and honestly about patterns of immoral and illegal behavior in particular communities. We can't close our eyes to the obvious. Drive-bys may be more common in black and Latino ghettos than in Lithuanian or Norwegian communities. And mob hits might be more common in Providence's Federal Hill than in Harlem's Sugar Hill. But, it should be apparent that such patterns have more to do with where criminals live—whether by choice or by circumstance—and, more important, where they do "business," than with the ethnic character of their consciences. Also, the concentration of crime in poor communities, many of these black, has more to do with economic and material suffering than ethical impoverishment. It makes no more sense to speak of the pathology of Italian communities because of the Mafia than it does to speak of the nihilism of Vietnamese communities because of the rise of gangs in such neighborhoods.

The moral viciousness of juvenocrats can be explained by their participation in illicit activities and immoral lifestyles that reinforce destructive behavior. As ethicists who study virtue have argued for centuries, moral health is encouraged by habits of thought and action that are repeatedly practiced. The same holds for vicious behavior. There's nothing endemic to black culture, versus, say, Jewish or Irish culture, that promotes vice. But there is something about the nature of a juvenocracy that encourages vicious behavior. In fact, a juvenocracy is explicitly organized around illicit, illegal, and immoral action. Its very purpose is to regularize such behavior. A juvenocracy shapes its actions so as to maximize the profits of its participants. Cutthroat, cold-hearted, vicious, and sometimes inhuman behavior—both toward other members of the juvenocracy and toward those outside its ranks—is not only common, it is crucial to the maintenance of the juvenocracy. Something like a Kantian moral imperative operates in the juvenocracy: stay safe, watch your homeboy's back, and make money at all costs. If one must make others unsafe, stab or shoot a neighbor in the back, or steal to "get paid," so be it. That's not an example of black nihilism any more than it's an example of white nihilism. And it's not a black ethic any more than it's a white ethic. It's an all too American ethic, (maybe even a universal one), one that unites a broader and deeper strand of folk than we're willing to admit. (Indeed, I've seen staggering nihilism in corporate America and in university communities, in certain businessmen for whom the buck was all, and in novelists whose narcissism and arrogance were a blight to behold.) The concepts of pathology and nihilism seem too class derived for my tastes. They stigmatize the very people who have the least resources to resist the sort of behavior for which the well-to-do are rarely held accountable.

Let me be clear. Vicious behaviors are no less vicious because they are rooted in generic factors of class, political economy, violence, and the like. But by getting a fix on how and why immoral behavior flourishes, we might have a better chance of figuring out what to do. On the one hand, if we believe the problem is cultural, we tell black folk to fix their cultures. We tell them to stop being pathological. Or if we believe they're nihilistic, we tell them to convert to love. On the other hand, if we think the problem flowers in black culture, but is rooted in complex economic, political, moral, and social factors, our answer is hugely different. A juvenocracy cannot be overcome by anything less than a radical reexamination of urban social policies, economic practices, and political measures aimed at black communities and black youth. A juvenocracy that thrives on violence, the political economy of drugs, and the culture of the gun must be viewed, in part, as a symptom of economic and racial injustice. It must also be seen as a moral surrender of black youth to the seductions of excessive material gratification. No amount of hand-wringing, navel gazing, or pulpit pounding about the good ol' black days will fix what's wrong. Black nostalgia for days when we were better simply won't do.

WITH THAT, WE END UP WHERE WE BEGAN: the rise of a juvenocracy has been complemented by the cultural fascination with, and revulsion to, the pop culture of black youth, especially hip-hop. For many critics, the two go hand in hand. But that's a mistaken perception. That's not to say that gangsta rappers, for instance, don't identify with real gangsters. That they don't feed off one another. That their styles and social aspirations are not easily confused. Still, most real gangsters don't listen to gangsta rap for inspiration to do what they do. They check out old-school grooves. Too many of them have said so for us to ignore it. A lot of gangsters prefer Al Green to Snoop Doggy Dogg. Too often, then, black youth are all lumped together—in the media, in discussions by black intellectuals, in the analyses of cultural critics, and in the public imagination.

Unlike Ralph Ellison's character in his famous novel, and the bulk of black folk for a long stretch of our history, black youth suffer, not from invisibility, but from *hypervisibility.* The surplus sighting, and citing, of young black bodies—in crime stories on the news, in congressional hearings about demeaning imagery in pop music, in shopping malls where they hang out, in police profiles where they are stigmatized, in suburban communities where they are surveilled—has draped paranoia and panic around their very limbs. In all the wrong ways, black youth are overexposed. (Is it any wonder, then, that they dress in oversize clothing to hide their demonized bodies, to diminish the measuring of their alleged menace?)

And unlike James Baldwin and generations of black folk, black youth don't suffer from namelessness. They suffer from *namefulness,* from too many names. The sheer name-ability of black youth, the ease with which they are misla-beled, promotes among black youth a negative solidarity, a unity produced by the attacks they have in common. Like Thomas Hobbes, black youth understand that human beings wield power through calling names and avoiding names. As Hobbes knew, black youth also know that names venerate and vilify. Names influence events. Hip-hop culture has provoked the naming, really the misnaming, of black youth: sadistic, self-destructive, violent, brutal, narcissistic, nihil-istic, pathological, immoral, and, for some, evil. Hip-hop has fought back. It uses strategies of naming, renaming, unnaming, and overnaming its own culture and the cultures—racist, rich, elite, bourgeois—against which it strives.

Instead of nostalgia, we need serious, rigorous analysis and critical appreciation of black youth. Instead of attacks on hip-hop culture, we need sharp, just, well-informed evaluations of its artistic statements and ethical imagination. Black nostalgia must be replaced by an even stronger force: the historic black determination to remain undefeated by pessimism from within black culture, and paranoia from beyond its borders. We must not be prisoners of our present circumstances, of current events. We must be prisoners of faith.

Such a lesson is helpful not only when dealing with our youth. It is equally true as we confront the perennial crisis of black leadership, and, more important, the exhausting demands of black followership. With the recent emergence of Colin Powell and Louis Farrakhan as credible black leaders, the nagging question of what route black folk should take into the next century—one of separation, or one of solidarity with other Americans—has renewed itself with foreboding intensity.

FIVE

Black Folk Lifted by Their Bootstraps Should Beware of Heels

The State of Black Leadership

> *In this period of transition and growing social change, there is a dire need for leaders who are calm and yet positive, leaders who avoid the extremes of "hotheadedness" and "Uncle Tomism." The urgency of the hour calls for leaders of wise judgment and sound integrity—leaders not in love with money, but in love with justice; leaders not in love with publicity, but in love with humanity; leaders who can subject their particular egos to the greatness of the cause.*
>
> Martin Luther King, Jr.
> "Facing the Challenge of a New Age," 1956

As I stood at the million man march, I felt the powerful waves of history wash over me. There's no denying that this march connected many of the men—more than a million, I believe—to a sense of racial solidarity that has largely been absent since the '60s. I took my son to Washington so that he could feel and see, drown in, even, an ocean of beautiful black brothers. I'd been speaking, talking, and writing about the problems of black men for years. I've got a brother and several nephews who are doing hard time in prison. I've got black male friends who are unemployed, uneducated, on welfare, without money or shelter, or behind bars. That is, the ones who aren't dead.

And so I went to the march, even critically defended it on *Nightline.* I went because I was desperate—yes desperate, a desperation that being a black intellectual or a black preacher can't stop, and that being a black father and brother only increases—to join with other black men who had a sense of the troubles black men face. I'd had enough of talking, although talking is better than exploding. I'd had enough of paying lip service to how bright, self-critical black men, had to get together to help put an end to the misery we've endured. And, yes, sometimes caused. I'd had enough of forums where the crises of black men were discussed at a safe distance from the pain those participating in the discussion wanted to end. I wanted to help highlight our economic and social suffering. I also wanted to help shoulder responsibility for how black men have mistreated black women, gays, and lesbians.

Besides, the goals of the march—registering thousands of new voters, encouraging direct political action, and raising money for black organizations—gave the gathering an exciting and practical purpose. True enough, the themes of the march—black men atoning for our ills, especially to black women, and taking responsibility for our own uplift—were complicated ideas that demanded more than a single gathering to successfully explore. But marches aren't primarily for analysis. They're for drama in the best sense. I viewed the march as a dramatizing of black men's willingness to share their heartbreaks and hopes with the world. I thought the march was a compelling way to get the ball rolling. I went to Washington with the hope that a larger, more insightful, more healthy, more self-critical, and more complex conversation about black men might get started.

In my hotel room the morning of the march, I caught Colin Powell on television explaining why he wouldn't be coming to Washington. Powell said that while he endorsed the purpose of the march—and why wouldn't he, since he is Mr. Responsibility twice over, as a military man and as a proud West Indian—he didn't want to give Louis Farrakhan legitimacy as a black leader. (That was a revealing comment indeed. For whom was Powell going to legitimate Farrakhan? Blacks? Probably not. They believe what they believe about Farrakhan without Powell's help. It was among whites, then, that Powell was concerned not to give Farrakhan too much play. What's intriguing—and I'll explore this in just a bit—is that whites already see a version of Farrakhan in Powell's brand of leadership, especially in the emphasis on personal responsibility.) At the time of the march, Powell was in the midst of a book tour to promote his newly published memoir. The hype over Powell's book had sparked the hopes of millions that he might run for the presidency. Powell's emergence as a leader to be reckoned with gave weight to his snub of Farrakhan, at least with a lot of whites.

I thought that morning about how Powell and Farrakahn's visibility raised issues other than the plight of black men. Their prominence renews debates about the role race plays in public life. Their newfound influence also provokes debates about the kind and quality of leaders black folk should have. For millions of blacks, of course, Powell is just the sort of leader we need: not too hung up on race, but still not ignorant of its harsh realities. Farrakhan, on the other hand, appeals to millions of blacks precisely because he's obsessed with race, with what it means to blacks and to whites. If Powell crosses over to whites, Farrakhan crosses them. And a lot of blacks as well. How do we explain Farrakhan's appeal to blacks, and the massive problems his leadership sharply symbolizes? My aim in this chapter is to figure that out. But to do that, we've got to first consider Farrakhan's rise in light of Powell's emergence, since both have come to represent widely divergent views on race in America.

To begin with, Powell's shrewd *un*candidacy, and Farrakhan's bid for mainstream leadership, have encouraged blacks to revisit an old dilemma: whether to bond with or separate from white America in the search for racial justice. Not that the choice is really that simple, or one that can in fact be made. It may be that the impossibility of divorcing America doesn't mean as much to separatists as the healthy self-definition they derive from being separatists, and that they and most blacks desperately desire. Despite its chauvinism and its romantic views of black culture, separatism gives many blacks the satisfaction—if wounded and childish—of white rejection. It says, simply: If you don't want to play with us, we don't want to play with you. Most blacks, no matter how much they love white folk, can identify with that feeling, have felt it on occasions too numerous to admit. The feeling even contains a surefire test to determine one's ideological bent. The blacks who get over such sentiments, especially in time for work the next day, are integrationists. The ones who don't recover are separatists. At least on paper.

Farrakhan and Powell are symbols of the divided mind of black America. Those of us who are integrationists want our cake of mainstream values. But many of us want to buy it from a black baker and eat it in a black restaurant in the black section of town. Others of us want our racial separatism. But we often want it in mixed company: a black dorm at a white university, a black history month in a predominantly white country, and a black house in a white suburb. The lure of separatism lingers because integration failed to provide the just society many blacks had hoped would arrive after the civil rights struggles of the '60s. But the failure of separatism is even greater. It has not delivered the *ethnitopia* it promises. That fact is often forgotten when black folk get angry at the slow pace of racial progress.

Their career paths certainly prove that Powell and Farrakhan think quite differently about race. In Powell's case, the glistening surface of his moderate views and military heroism reflects our deepest desires to *transcend* race. Farrakhan's attempted leap from the fringes to the front line of black life captures the disappointment with mainstream black leadership. It captures as well the desire to *translate* race into the dialect of black experience. But when it comes to rehabilitating black culture, Powell's transcendence of race and Farrakhan's translation of race may be, in some ways, flip sides of the same coin. For instance, both agree that self-help is key to black redemption. They also want to restore conservative cultural values in black families and in American society.

This is partly due to their common West Indian roots. Farrakhan and Powell were reared by parents who valued hard work. Their parents also prized Caribbean beliefs about blacks working among themselves to create a stronger society. In Powell's case, that vision extends out from his black family to embrace the entire nation. Powell believes blacks should fully participate in American democracy. That belief is rooted in his desire to see the brilliant diversity of a predominantly black Caribbean culture come alive, not only for black Americans, but for the entire United States.

Farrakhan's beliefs about black self-determination are rooted in fellow West Indian Marcus Garvey's separatist doctrines. Farrakhan's desire to create a black ethnitopia is rooted in Garvey's notion of black self-help and racial solidarity. Farrakhan is also attracted to Garvey's vision of black Americans finding their true destiny in solidarity with Africans around the globe, free from the shackles of white supremacy. It is not surprising that Powell and Farrakhan argue for radically different paths to racial salvation. What is intriguing is that they may have more than calypso and color in common. Powell is, perhaps, more rooted in black culture than his public image lets on. Farrakhan may be more closely tied to mainstream America than he or his followers care to confess. The transcendence and the translation of race, while certainly discrete, converge at crucial points.

BEFORE HE DECIDED NOT TO RUN for the presidency, Colin Powell was a compelling figure for many whites because of the hope that he could heal racial conflicts by transcending race. His appeal as a potential racial healer had barely taken hold when the verdicts from the Simpson trial raised the stakes of Powell's crossover ambitions. Before the Simpson verdicts, the general's political appeal depended on his rejection of racial bad faith. For many Americans, racial bad faith was viewed as resistance to the politics of radical integration. After the verdict, Powell's plausibility as a presidential candidate depended on a negative charisma: his ability to portray the transcendence of race as the suppression of race. For many whites, nothing short of Powell's rejection of any sort of racial solidarity with blacks would prove satisfying. (He faced the same dilemma of race transcendence as the black Simpson jurors discussed in chapter 1.) Where there is a conflict between racial and national identity, race loses its power to hold the trust or interest of those outside its ranks. Why? Because black identity, at least, is seen as particular, and, therefore, limited. The transcendence, or suppression, of black identity becomes the condition for its survival. This is the paradox that Powell's success both reinforces and obscures.

Unlike Simpson, however, Powell has refused to ignore his race. Nevertheless, Powell has worked against the brutal confinements of bigotry to prove his worth. Now Powell lurks in the unconscious of many whites as an O.J. replacement. He is seen by many as a "Nice Negro" who must extend the illusion of colorlessness to prove his gratitude for being allowed to live the American dream. In fact, as Simpson's example has shown, the cost of colorlessness is always an investment in whiteness. African-Americans can never effectively transcend race by remaining black. Whites, however, rarely need to get beyond their race to insure their acceptance as authentic Americans. Whiteness is already viewed as a universal identity. To be successful with many whites, Powell-the-presidential-candidate would have had to finish the job of Ideal Negro that O.J. failed to complete. More painfully, Powell would have had to atone for the fateful rejection of a transcendent American identity symbolized in the jurors' decision.

(As a nation, we rarely feel the need to transcend white-ness. There is little language available to even express the idea. To be sure, we want to get beyond the bad effects of whiteness—slavery, racism, and so on. But we rarely want to get beyond whiteness per se. With blacks, such a distinction is collapsed. To get beyond race, to transcend it, really expresses the national need to get beyond blackness per se. Blackness per se has been so completely identified with negative attributes—limited, narrow, particular—that we can rarely imagine it representing a universal ideal. One might say, "Wait a minute, look at Michael Jordan, the best basketball player on the globe. He's a black man whom everybody wants to be. He doesn't have to stop being black to be great." True. But Jordan is admired precisely because his blackness is never an issue; it is never referenced in a way to threaten the dominant society. If, like Muslim ballplayer Mahmoud Abdul-Rauf, he challenged the codes of whiteness or the conventions of dominant culture, his blackness would become an issue. As long as blackness is not an issue, that is, as long as it doesn't make a difference, as long as it's suppressed, contained, or controlled, it's alright.)

Despite his decision not to run for the presidency, Powell's heroic flair continues to rivet us. There is still a great deal of fascination with the "real" Colin Powell behind the Public Man. Powell is valued by blacks and whites because he appears able to overcome the deficits of race. Interestingly, however, Powell can also speak of the bitter memory of race as a means to defeat its frustrating persis-tence. Unlike Johnnie Cochran, whose attempt to speak of race was viewed by many whites as divisive, Powell's use of race is seen as an attempt to forge racial harmony. The difference in perception has a lot to do with how Powell's life story embodies classic American myths of self-invention and individualism.

Powell's story combines elements of racial mythology with ideals of national character. His personal immigrant's tale highlights and reinforces the defining features of American identity. Powell heroically turned the liabilities of race to great advantage. He conquered racism as a military hero, and in that role he shined the (often diminished) brilliance of black American life into foreign lands and into closed minds closer to home. Powell's focus on the American dream sometimes blinds him to America's nightmares. But the general is also capable of a sober reveille: he knows the costs of denied opportunity. In the magical arc of Powell's triumphant patriotism, Frederick Douglass elbows Thomas Jefferson for a spot at Eisenhower's side.

For many whites, Powell is how the American dream looks when it wears black. For them, his strong endorsement of American citizenship neutralizes the strong suspicions blacks possess of unqualified loyalty to our country. Powell's heroism is rooted in military service and the moral discipline that we like to believe comes with the territory. He eases the fears of many whites who view black masculinity as a symbol of moral chaos and social disorder. If Powell loomed as a potential political savior, it is in large part because he appeared to bleach the dangerous elements of black masculinity in the curing pool of patriotism.

For instance, near the end of his memoir, *My American Journey,* there is a scene that perfectly captures how Colin Powell appears to transcend the deadly consequences of black masculinity and race even as he embodies their urgent contradictions. By 1989, Powell had become, at age 52, the first black and youngest ever Chairman of the Joint Chiefs of Staff. He still held that position in 1992, when rioting broke out in Los Angeles following the acquittal of four policemen charged with beating Rodney King. The riots were a brutal reminder of this nation's still inflamed racial passions. Powell was sick with disbelief.

"It can't be happening," he recalls thinking. "It was nearly 35 years since President Eisenhower had sent troops into Little Rock to quell the violence over school integration…" Now Powell, a latter-day Eisenhower of sorts, was being ordered by George Bush to place a federalized National Guard under a central command. It was an ironic and bittersweet symbol of racial progress that a black man was now responsible for containing the chaos of black rage and rebellion. But there's more.

As Powell watched the riots blaze on television, he received a call from national security adviser Brent Scowcroft to help shape President Bush's response in a speech to be given the night the catastrophe struck. The draft of Bush's remarks that Powell viewed had "the fingerprints of the far right all over" it, with its insistence that "the rioting was criminal" and with its failure to recognize that "the violence had not incubated in isolation" but that it had "deep social roots." Powell urged White House Chief of Staff Sam Skinner to get some "reconciliation into the President's message."

That night, Powell felt vindicated as Bush tempered his call for law and order with an acknowledgment that King's beating was "revolting," and that our nation must "offer a better future to minority Americans." Powell caught Bush's speech that night in an empty room in Washington's Grand Hyatt Hotel, where the general was attending the annual Horatio Alger scholarship dinner. Such incongruities have shaped Powell's destiny from the start.

Powell's West Indian roots explain, perhaps, the huge investment he has made in the immigrant's belief that

America is a land of unbridled potential. Powell is aware that such sentiments wear thin on American blacks. Powell admits that his parents chose to emigrate to this country for the same reason that Italians, Irish, and Hungarians did: to seek a better life with their families. But he knows that American blacks have a far different emotional and psychological relationship to a nation where they were brought in chains. Still, Powell sometimes chides American blacks for not possessing his perpetual optimism. Such optimism is not what many blacks feel. Instead, they shield hard-earned faith and hope from the superficial enthusiasms of positive thinking.

But then, Powell's optimism was fed by his uncommon good fortune and hard work. He skyrocketed to success in the military, often achieving higher ranks early and with distinction. Commissioned out of college, Lieutenant Powell was sent in 1958 to Georgia's Fort Benning, where for the first time he faced the South and its racism head-on. Powell has written that "racism was still relatively new to me, and I had to find a way to cope psychologically...I was not going to allow someone else's feelings about me to become my feelings about myself." Powell fought racism with humor and steely resolve, acknowledging his hurt and anger, but mostly feeling challenged. "I'll show you!" was his attitude.

For the most part, though, his criticisms of the Army are eclipsed by his gratitude for the benefits the military gives to minorities. In Powell's perspective, the Army was living the democratic ideal ahead of the rest of America. Since the '50s, Powell argues, the Army has had less discrimination, a truer merit system, and leveler playing fields than existed in any Southern city hall or Northern corporation.

Powell ripped through the Army's ranks with remarkable speed. He was blessed by the sort of good luck that gives talent its best chance to shine. Powell served a second tour in Vietnam. And he sharpened his soldier's credentials in Germany, Korea, and at assorted sites in the states. But the corridors of political power is where Powell has shined his halo of power and prestige. Powell was sent by the Army to George Washington University to earn a Master of Business Administration degree in 1969, when he was 32. Soon after he became a White House Fellow, apprenticing under Frank Carlucci and Caspar Weinberger at the Office of Management and Budget. Powell was certainly on the fast track when he attended the National War College and when he served as military assistant to four secretaries of defense, including Carlucci and Weinberger as well as Harold Brown and Richard Cheney. He was Carlucci's assistant when Carlucci became Ronald Reagan's national security adviser. Finally, he was named Reagan's sixth national security adviser before assuming his duties as the Chairman of the Joint Chiefs of Staff.

The fact that Powell's career flourished away from the precincts of pure military service sticks in his craw. It's not that Powell missed any wars in the '70s and '80s, but his posts during those years for the most part consisted of a series of jobs inside the beltway. For insiders like Powell, military service makes an authentic soldier. The perception among his peers that he is a "political general," a bureaucrat whose battles took place within Washington's beltway, cuts deeply at his view of himself. Ironically, his very chumminess with politicos, gained in exile from the thrills and traumas of the battlefield, helped Powell a great deal. That was obvious as he mastered the military and political dimensions of the Gulf War. A keen knowledge of the political scene has also allowed Powell to horn in on the elitist populism that has been Ross Perot's specialty. Powell as homeboy doesn't quite work. But Powell as Honest Abe reborn has generated a certain low-key glamor.

In the end, Colin Powell may be one of the last great moderates. Ideally, a moderate tries to take stock of independent thinking in arriving at a course of action. But there's the rub. Political history has shown that in our nation the moderates end up looking like and voting with the conservatives more than the radicals. Powell's moderation is attractive to many whites because of the powerful way it symbolizes the transcendence of race. The transcendence of race is crucial because it allows the bitter history of race to be overcome. But it also depends on a highly selective use of the facts of race.

Powell's transcendence of race is made possible by a key factor: the perception that race is not his overriding concern. As a result, the scope of the lessons he is able to teach is limited by a need to preserve the illusion of transcending race. An "excessive" emphasis on race shatters that illusion. In these terms, race can only be overcome by being underrepresented. The explicit expression of race—even to point to its persistence—can only occur in a context where the intent is to quickly move beyond race. There is no loitering allowed on the premises of race. Neither are substantive, uncomfortable explorations of race permitted. To discuss the facts of race is only acceptable if one points to the progress that has been made by comparing the present to the past.

Of course, it's alright to use race to suggest that we have a long way to go because espousing this view is part of the containment, and suppression, of racial conflict. How? It is a way of reducing disturbing realities to cliché. Of course everyone knows that the state of race is not perfect. Therefore, when Powell repeats this, as he has, it's no big deal. In fact, by now it's common knowledge. That's a way of deflecting attention from the more disturbing features of present racism. It is also a shrewd way of obscuring the link between the context and subtext of race. Powell's wife, Alma, uncovered that link when she openly admitted that she didn't want her husband running for the presidency because of the racist hate mail he had received. Her statement wasn't simply a matter of pointing out how bad racism had been in the past. Neither was hers a "racism still exists but there's been tremendous progress" story. Alma Powell exposed the terror of the present threat of racism. By doing this, she "outed" race transcendence as a strategy that has masked the ongoing pain of race. She blew the cover off the illusion of race transcendence by her husband.

The transcendence of race remains a powerful dream to many whites because it suppresses the bitter memory of race. It would also relieve whites of the hard work that must be done in the present to make things right. Powell's patriotism and conservative values might have taken him a long way with many whites and blacks. But his version of race transcendence also turned off many blacks. The polls taken during the period Powell was considering a presidential run showed he had greater pull among whites than among blacks. Farrakhan's recent rise to black mainstream prominence must be viewed against this backdrop. In crucial ways, Farrakhan is the blackened version of Powell's conservative cultural beliefs and social values. Anyone doubting this judgment need look no further than Farrakhan's attempt to broaden his leadership with the Million Man March.

WHILE IT MAY BE DIFFICULT on the surface to discern Farrakhan's truck with Powell's moderate conservatism, they share a crucial assumption about the mechanisms of black improvement: pulling oneself up by the bootstraps. While Powell sees self-help as key to transcending race, Farrakhan sees it as key to translating race into the idiom of black self-determination. Undoubtedly, such an emphasis, as I argued above, flows from their common ethnic roots. In Farrakhan's case, his roots are cloaked in virtually the same sort of secrecy that shrouds the internal workings of the Nation of Islam. To get a sense of Farrakhan's translation of race, and his appeal to millions of blacks, we'll have to understand where he came from and what forces shaped him.

Born in the Bronx in 1933, Farrakhan, like Powell, was the child of West Indian immigrants. He fed from his mother Mae Manning's Saint Kitts roots (formerly a British crown colony) and drank in his stepfather Louis Walcott's Barbados heritage. But from the beginning, there was trouble. Mae fell in love with a Jamaican, Percival Clark, who quickly departed after their marriage. Still wed to Clark, Mae met Louis Walcott, who fathered Farrakhan's older half brother Alvan Walcott. Clark reemerged long enough to get Mae pregnant with another child, only to disappear again. The conflict was cruel: Mae was legally married to Clark, but in love with Walcott. Mae's predicament was compounded by the fact that she and Alvan were dark. She was afraid that her baby would be fair-skinned, proving her infidelity. She tried desperately to abort the child three times with a coat hanger. When her efforts failed, she decided to have the baby, born Louis Eugene Walcott, now Louis Farrakhan, in 1933. Later, the elder Walcott would abandon the family as well.

Farrakhan was brought up in Boston, in Roxbury, a black section of town permeated by West Indian culture. Showing early signs of musical promise, Farrakhan took up the violin at the age of five, eventually gaining admission to Boston

Latin, then arguably the most prestigious public school in America. He experimented with the guitar and the ukulele as well. Farrakhan also played for the Boston College Orchestra and won the *Ted Mack Original Amateur Hour.* Reared as an Episcopalian, he was deeply influenced by the black nationalist teaching of his pastor, Nathan Wright, and the Garveyite doctrine of black self-determination, popular in his home and throughout Roxbury.

Although he had aspirations to attend Juilliard, Farrakhan's poor background (his mother worked as a domestic) placed the school far beyond his grasp. Instead, Farrakhan attended Winston-Salem Teachers College (now Winston-Salem State University) in North Carolina for a couple of years after graduating from high school. He moved back to Boston and married his pregnant high-school sweetheart, Betsey, now Khadidja, in 1953. But his musical interests continued. Like his mother, Farrakhan was a fan of calypso. Many of the music's masters—including Lord Executioner, Growler, Attila the Hun, and Black Prince—found their way to the Walcott home in Roxbury. Similar to strands of hip-hop culture that would later regard Farrakhan as a hero, calypso fused art and politics. Like hip-hop, calypso was grounded in a specific cultural moment of black masculine expression: it grew from a Trinidadian Lenten festival where men competed with one another to signify in clever ways on the dominant culture and its power. Calypso's lessons would certainly not be lost on Farrakhan. He ascended the ladder of power and influence within the Nation of Islam while doing rhetorical battle with white supremacy.

Farrakhan himself eventually gained local fame as a calypso singer, performing as Calypso Gene and as The Charmer. In the early '50s Farrakhan's nightclub career put him into position to meet Malcolm X, who was proselytizing in a

Boston club. But it was in 1955, when he was in Chicago to perform at a club, that Farrakhan was invited to a Savior's Day Convention to hear Elijah Muhammad. He immediately converted to the Nation of Islam. When he returned to Boston, his charm was wrapped in a brand-new moniker that rivaled the intrigue of his stage name: Louis X.

His gifts in the secular world aided Farrakhan's rise in the Nation. He continued to write songs, and penned two plays, one of which, *The Trial*, brought him fame among his fellow converts. The play also earned him notoriety outside the Nation when lines from it—especially "I charge you [the white man] with being the greatest liar on earth"—were featured in Mike Wallace's now famous 1959 documentary of the Nation, entitled "The Hate That Hate Produced."

Farrakhan's first assignment was to Temple #7, in Harlem, where he soon became assistant to Malcolm X. Because of his organizational talent and oratorical gifts, Farrakhan then became Captain of the Fruit of Islam, the defense arm of the Nation of Islam, at the Nation's Boston Mosque, and was named the Minister shortly thereafter. Working his way through the ranks of the Nation, Farrakhan eventually became Minister of Harlem's Temple #7, and then National Representative for the Honorable Elijah Muhammad after mentor-turned-mortal-enemy Malcolm X's bitter secession in 1964.

Since the late '60s, Farrakhan's reputation has continued to grow, even outside of the Nation. He draws thousands of blacks to venues around the country promoting a message of black rage at white supremacy. Despite his undeniable success in reviving and reshaping the Nation of Islam, Farrakhan has been covered by a veil of suspicion that he cannot remove: that he had a hand in Malcolm's death. That belief has been publicly expressed by Malcolm's widow,

Dr. Betty Shabazz, on many occasions since her husband's death in 1965. It was strong enough nearly 30 years after Malcolm's assassination to leave Malcolm's daughter, Qubilah Shabazz, vulnerable to a plot to kill Farrakhan in 1994. (That latter event led to a public rapprochement between Farrakhan and Dr. Shabazz at Harlem's Apollo Theater in 1995.)

For many other critics as well, Farrakhan's rise to leadership is bathed in Malcolm's blood, although there's no proof that he had a direct tie to Malcolm's assassination. Farrakhan has confessed that he certainly helped create the atmosphere that led to Malcolm's death. Malcolm's assassination came after his break with the Nation and his claim that Muhammad held back the black revolution by forbidding aggressive social action. Yet what provoked the Nation's greatest contempt was Malcolm's charge that Muhammad had committed adultery with several Muslim women. In a 1964 issue of *Muhammad Speaks,* the publication of the Nation of Islam, Farrakhan wrote the now infamous words:

> Only those who wish to be led to hell, or to their doom, will follow Malcolm. The die is set, and Malcolm shall not escape, especially after such evil, foolish talk about his benefactor…Such a man as Malcolm is worthy of death and would have been met with death if it had not been for Muhammad's confidence in Allah for victory over his enemies.

But Farrakhan has stated that the FBI had a hand in Malcolm's death as well. Indeed, FBI files indicate that its agents were aware of death threats against Malcolm within the Nation. But they failed to warn Malcolm or to protect him from such threats. Given their history of vicious behavior, it is quite easy to believe that the FBI might have been involved in Malcolm's murder. (After all, in the early '70s the FBI would infiltrate the Chicago Black Panther Party, instigating and directly participating in the assassinations of Party leaders Mark Clark and Fred Hampton.) It is a bitter irony, one that underscores the self-defeating habits of many black nationalist groups, that either the NOI or the FBI, or both, are plausible culprits in Malcolm's death. Just because Malcolm's assassination was carried out by members of the Nation does not release the FBI from its role in Malcolm's death. In the same vein, Farrakhan is not freed from guilt by association, even if he didn't pull the trigger or give the orders to murder Malcolm.

It is telling that two of our most brilliant black leaders, Jesse Jackson and Louis Farrakhan, have blood issues—relating to mothers and mentors—hanging over their heads. Each is held responsible for acts that seem intensely Greek. They are viewed as both exalting and erasing their spiritual fathers. Each is accused of Oedipal gestures aimed at avenging their mothers of distant, deserting fathers while charting their own glorification.

A lot of ink has been spilled in efforts to figure out the effect on Jackson's psyche of learning as a child that the man married to his mother was not his father. Jackson's mother got pregnant by her married next-door neighbor when she was a teen. Jackson grew up stigmatized by his ambiguous paternity. This fact is said to needle Jackson's ego and to drive him to seek acceptance and the limelight. Compounding the issue of his paternity is the unproved claim that Jackson dipped his hands in Martin Luther King's freshly spilled blood and wiped it on his shirt to prove his closeness to the slain leader and to legitimate his ascension as King's heir. No matter what brilliance Jackson has since achieved, and despite some accomplishments that King himself might have been incapable of pulling off, Jackson's alleged act follows him. It is viewed as a betrayal of King's spirit of sacrifice and selflessness.

Farrakhan, too, has an issue with his paternity. The very lightness of his skin is the sign of Farrakhan's having been fathered under unusual circumstances. There is much speculation, too, about Farrakhan's light skin making him extraordinarily conscious of color. Some critics see that color consciousness as the force behind Farrakhan's relentless efforts to be black beyond black, to strike a chord of authenticity that leaves little doubt as to his racial identity. This might be psychobabble. If it is true, however, it certainly places Farrakhan in league with Malcolm X, who was similarly tortured by his light complexion.

Strangely enough, the shadow of doubt about Farrakhan's role in Malcolm's death is only increased by his denials. That has to do, in part, with the suspicion of those who "doth protest too much." Then too, it might be because Farrakhan's denials of direct participation in Malcolm's death allow him to draw subtle benefits. Each time he admits that he whipped up the atmosphere that led to Malcolm's death, Farrakhan reinforces his good standing among Nation loyalists who still view Malcolm as a traitor. By consistently denying his direct participation in Malcolm's death, he pleases many who view Malcolm as a hero. So Farrakhan is able to satisfy Malcolm's enemies and many of his friends and followers with the same disclaimers. It is unclear if Farrakhan's denials are genuine or if they are shrewd calypso counter-strategies designed to deflect criticism.

His disputes with Malcolm aside, Farrakhan has proved to be a brilliant twin to the personality Malcolm shaped in the Nation of Islam. Farrakhan is one-half the fulfillment of Malcolm's divided mind about which route—separatist or limited solidarity with progressive whites—black folk should take to survive in America. If Farrakhan is Malcolm's shadow self—at least the half of Malcolm that was disdainful of white folk while he was in the Nation, and cautious about proceeding with their help once he departed—Farrakhan aggressively shields himself from Malcolm's brighter, perhaps blinding, other half. That half of Malcolm believed that caste and class should be attacked as well as race. That half of Malcolm believed that black folk should be open to socialist, humanitarian, and democratic strategies for racial uplift. That half of Malcolm believed that white folk really weren't devils. Farrakhan totes his contempt for that other side of Malcolm around his neck as a talisman. It wards off the amnesia that Farrakhan believes clouds black prophets once they go soft. It is a reminder to Farrakhan of the price black leaders pay once they lose their way in a racial wilderness where they are lured by misty dreams of cooperating with the enemy.

If Malcolm is a burden to Farrakhan, representing both a past Farrakhan seeks to forget and the potential for a more reconciliatory future he prays won't arrive, Malcolm's presence is also, strangely, a blessing. Why? Because Farrakhan is able to spook white folk by reprising the nerve-rattling, fear-inducing bogeyman act that Malcolm ingeniously put on as Elijah Muhammad's spokesman. Unlike Malcolm, though, Farrakhan won't foil the punch line by repenting in the end. It is a job for which Farrakhan is supremely suited.

Like all of the Nation's great prophets, Farrakhan has a gift for painting the ugliness of white supremacy. In fact, it was the Nation's ingenuity for mining the resentments and unfulfilled fantasies of the black poor—a charm that worked even better for Marcus Garvey—that drew so many huddled, teeming black masses from skid rows, dens of iniquity, prisons, and enslavement to drugs to the Nation's statutes of liberty. The most shining example was Malcolm Little, later Malcolm X. Allah's Messenger Elijah Muhammad gave the Nation of Islam an institutional life that drew from the shadowy inspiration of founder W.D. Fard. Malcolm put the organization on the map, and on the minds of Americans far beyond the Nation's golden-era hundred thousand members in the '60s. Malcolm's orations, while built on the Messenger's teachings, brilliantly reworked the Nation's esoteric theology into a coherent assault on the absurdity of white supremacy. With Malcolm's loss, the Nation lacked for a public moralist through whose intellectual arteries the blood of revelation from the Messenger might flow.

With Elijah Muhammad's death in 1975, the mantle of leadership fell to his son, Wallace D. Muhammad, later Warithuddin Deen Muhammad. But the younger Muhammad led the Nation into orthodox Islam. Although his father had begun the process, Muhammad's revelation to the Nation was even more radical: that its racialist outlook no longer squared with the religious beliefs of universalism and color-blindness practiced by orthodox Islam. Plus, the increasing class status of many black Muslims—they jumped from poverty to the middle class in a generation—gave them a compelling reason to go mainstream. Their theology followed their pocketbooks. Thus, the Nation of Islam became the World Community of al-Islam in the West (WCIW), and two years later, the American Muslim Mission.

Within three years, however, Farrakhan left Muhammad's mainstream Islamic group, which now has nearly three million members. Farrakhan resurrected the Nation of Islam in 1978. He awakened its members with his fresh interpretations of old Nation beliefs. That separatism is salvation. That black rage is righteous. That the poor are not mere pariahs.

That prisoners are potential princes. And that black folk are God's real chosen people. These were the pillars of Farrakhan's translation of race into the language of black self-determination and resistance to white supremacy.

Farrakhan's three-year exile taught him how easy it was for the Messenger's beliefs to be attacked or ignored. He set out to update and extend Elijah Muhammad's influence by pumping apocalyptic thunder into the Nation's eschatology. In Christian circles, eschatology has to do with the matters of ultimate importance: death, hell, heaven, the Last Judgment, the matters that come at the end of existence when God sums up human history and metes out punishment or reward. The notion of realized eschatology is the belief that those issues seep into time right now, that they cannot be put off by appeals to heaven or hell beyond history. Something like realized eschatology, perhaps more suitably termed a blues eschatology, is at work in the Nation's theological undercurrents. This blues eschatology drenches history in the crisis of black identity and gives the suffering and salvation of black folk a cosmic meaning.

For Farrakhan, black people are the world's Original People. What affects them affects the universe. The world is in Allah's hands. Black people, who are separated by degree, not kind, from Allah, are themselves divine. Hence, the judgment that black people declare, when they have been saved from their slavish dependence on the white world, is itself the foretaste, and the partial fulfillment, of a divine judgment. Under a blues eschatology, the events of black life take on an apocalyptic weight. Black suffering is placed at the heart of existence. The suffering of the black poor, victims of white racist violence, black males, and black leaders are all charged with a surplus of religious emotion. In fact, attempting to harm them is attempting to harm God.

Farrakhan has given the beliefs of Elijah Muhammad a face-lift. The white devil demonology has been largely replaced by blistering, bitter attacks on the practice of white supremacy. And while the Nation's apolitical stance has been replaced by strategic participation in black politics, Farrakhan has also extended Muhammad's reach into the Islamic world on the Nation's own terms. Farrakhan's coziness with a dictator like Iraq's Saddam Hussein is explained by Hussein's support of Farrakhan's relentless attacks on America's racist imperialism. It is also made possible by a solidarity forged by religious beliefs. Of course, one must question Farrakhan's embrace of Hussein in light of the exploitative manner in which Hussein, a secular nationalist, threw off the official anti-Islamic policy in Iraq to consolidate his power and influence by wooing the religious devotees of Islam.

During the '50s, Elijah Muhammad had become friendly with North Africa's Gamal Abdel Nasser. Farrakhan has forged a controversial alliance with his star pupil, Libyan dictator Mu'ammar Qaddafi. Both Qaddafi's political perspective and patronage (millions of dollars since the late '70s) are important to Farrakhan. Qaddafi's famous *Green Book or Third Universal Theory* presents an alternative to both capitalism and communism. This partially explains Farrakhan's poor translation (or is it a good translation of Qaddafi's unworkable theory?) of Qaddafi's philosophy in Farrakhan's militant rhetoric against the state even as he supports versions of black capitalism.

Even in light of his forays into the Muslim world, Farrakhan's 1996 visit to Africa and the Middle East proved deeply problematic. Farrakhan offered no public criticism of African nations and Islamic countries involved in unjust political practices. This raises serious questions about his commitment to justice, his moral judgment, and his ability to provide the sort of self-critical leadership so sorely needed among black Americans. Farrakhan visited Nigeria, pleading with human rights advocates to give dictator General Sani Abacha three more years to make good on his promise to return civilian rule to the African country. Farrakhan overlooked the detention of hundreds of prodemocracy activists without trial, and the executions of opposition leaders like poet Ken Saro-Wiwa. Farrakhan, it seems, sanctified the barbarous practices of an African nation for no other reason than that the nation is black. Farrakhan reminded Nigerians that stern discipline was sometimes necessary, and that Moses, like Abacha, had been a dictator as well.

In Tehran, Farrakhan vowed to help the mullahs in their bid to overthrow the "Great Satan," the United States. Farrakhan has in the past been the guest of Sudanese leaders Bashir and Turabi in Khartoum. On his last visit to the Sudan, Farrakhan heaped praise on the Sudanese government, lauding its "wise Islamic leadership." But there has been a recent surge of slavery in the Sudan. Farrakhan said nothing. Worse still, the Sudanese government has wiped out hundreds of thousands of its people in a bitter civil war. Still, Farrakhan said nothing. Grievous, too, is the allegation that when Mohamed Athie of the International Coalition Against Chattel Slavery sought to speak for Africans enslaved in the Sudan at the Million Man March, his request was ignored.

Such behavior trumps Farrakhan's bid for mainstream black leadership. The tragedy is that his behavior occurred *after* the Million Man March, where Farrakhan made a credible if controversial claim to the leadership of millions of blacks. Farrakhan's actions after the Million Man March highlight nagging questions that emerged in the build-up to the gathering. Can a leader who has preached separatist dogma unite a broad spectrum of black Americans in their quest for social justice? Can the head of an authoritarian, some have said fascist, organization that thrives on racial conspiracies, bizarre gnostic beliefs, and religious charisma yield to the demands of a democratic constituency? Will Farrakhan's non-Muslim followers be free to criticize him? Or will they live in fear of being beat up or silenced by loyalists who consider such criticism blasphemous? These questions all point, perhaps, to a more basic question. Is race translation superior to race transcendence? Or, to put it another way, do the virtues of race translation outweigh the obvious deficits of a leadership built on race transcendence? The Million Man March provides a vehicle to explore the good, bad, and ugly aspects of race translation.

There are those who reviled the march as a "swamp of hatred." Others have romanticized it. I experienced a more ambiguous reality. The march embodied and cast light on complex cultural conflicts in black life over masculinity, ethnocentrism, responsibility, and atonement. It also highlighted the strengths and weaknesses of leadership built on race translation. Only a fool would fail to understand why many women, gays, lesbians, Jews, whites, and blacks were troubled by this march. I can also understand why they remain troubled by the place of Louis Farrakhan in black political life. In the lively contest to define the emerging black culture that this march symbolizes, these are issues that cannot be sidestepped.

The Million Man March is a logical extension, and a brilliant summing up, of Farrakhan's vocation of translating race. The Million Man March clarified how Farrakhan's leadership has translated race with a heavy masculine accent. Masculine forms of experience. Masculine journeys to self-definition. Masculine quests for freedom. Masculine struggles for manhood. The Nation's genius—and its grave limitation too—has always been its yen to redeem black masculinity. This is a theme that has only recently caught fire among pundits, practitioners, prophets, and public intellectuals. But Farrakhan was way ahead of the game. Another way of stating this is to say that the Nation's and Farrakhan's vice—a focus on men, leading to forms of sexism and paternalism—has been their virtue. That virtue is realized in Farrakhan's foresight that the problems of black male life would come to dominate the moral landscapes of black communities.

Farrakhan's foresight was both prophecy and patriarchy. It is now a fact that black men's problems do affect entire black communities. But it is equally true that the Nation's patriarchal emphasis has contributed to the troublesome effects of black masculinity. Some have made the dangerous argument that because the Nation of Islam's masculine obsession has put it in a good position to do something about black male problems, black patriarchy is a valuable force. But by placing black men at the center of its universe, the Nation neglected the lives, pains, and perspectives of black women. Plus, it failed to acknowledge the lethal effects of such masculine obsession on black women: the devaluation of black women's minds and bodies in misogyny, physical abuse, female submission, and the like.

At the same time it is true that the Nation's patriarchal practices blind feminists, political progressives, and others to the help and insight the Nation might offer black males. In that case, the insularity for which the Nation is attacked is true of those groups as well.

The Nation's singular focus on helping black men get their lives together is driven by its ideology of resistance to white supremacy. The Nation has worked diligently to make proud men out of black prisoners, those in jail or those whose self-image is distorted because they are captives to a worship of the white world. The Nation has always seen black male addictions—whether to violence, drugs, or white acceptance—as symptoms of a virus of lostness which infects the entire black community. The Nation holds that the lostness of black men leads them to abuse their wives or children; to abuse their bodies with alcohol or bad food; to maim or murder each other; and to embrace, like black revolutionary theorist Frantz Fanon, the breasts of white womanhood in search of the milk of affection and affirmation. Long before the decline of black male life became widely apparent, and long before black males were vilified and glamorized by both the cultural right and the left, the Nation of Islam preached its own brand of salvation for black males. And from the very beginning, the core of the Nation's message has not changed. They believe that black men can only be saved by being restored as loving leaders in black families where they receive and return adoration and respect.

With good reason, that message was strongly criticized by black feminists leading up to the march as a thin cover for patriarchal posturing. Seeking to restore the black man as the head of the family devalues families where black women, by chance or choice, run the show. In the Nation's (and Newt Gingrich's) view, such families are defective until the black man returns to rule—and serve—in full glory by spreading his masculine splendor. And, no doubt, more of his seed. This deeply conservative vision of the black family, one held, perhaps, by millions of blacks, has blinded us to all sorts of nontraditional families where health and prosperity reign. This is no argument against the nuclear family's virtues, of which there are many. It is just a cautionary note against making it the only viable model for our communities. It is easy to see how feminist critics believe the language of black male restoration has only deepened the problems of black males and black communities. It makes women and girls minor factors in the equation of racial redemption. For such critics, the Million Man March would be business as usual. It would be a crude throwback to the times when women were expected to stay on the sidelines to cheer on men in the work of thinking, acting, and leading.

There is, however, a crucial difference between acknowledging the specific pains of black males—and hence drawing dramatic attention to the resources and remedies for their problems—and old-fashioned, if slickly updated, attempts to ignore the lives of black girls and women. Unfortunately, the two have often been collapsed. I agree with critics who argue that the rhetoric of black male suffering is often cobbled together from a distortion of black female troubles. Thus, the very language of black male crisis erases black women's faces and bodies from the canvas of social suffering. It is simply not true that black men's hurts are more important than the social horrors black women face. Too often, however, black male advocates behave and speak as if that's the case. What is undeniable is that the problems that hurt poor, young, black males—problems linked to the juvenocracies I described in chapter 4—affect the health and character of the communities in which these males live, and, too often, where they die. It is the immediacy and impact of black male problems on our national life, not their greater importance, that justify attention to their plight.

There is much to be said for black women standing side by side with black men to address the problems of black males. This is especially true because black women and children often bear the brunt of black men's rage. Black women's and children's bodies are often convenient targets for an aggression that black men fail to usefully direct toward the forces that cause their pain. Black women have energetically, and often without acknowledgment, fashioned solutions to the suffering of black males. They have done so as mothers, sisters, daughters, nieces, aunts, grandmothers, social workers, social critics, domestics, factory laborers, historians, doctors, civil rights leaders, and on and on.

Still, there are some things that black men have got to do by and for themselves. There exists among black men a great hunger for responsibility. That concept, often with good cause, is viewed with skepticism by the left, including feminists and black progressives. It's not that the left doesn't want people to be responsible. But it knows that for responsibility to make sense, for it to be a just way to judge individuals, we must account for the social forces stacked against those from whom we expect responsible behavior. In this light, there is truth to feminist arguments that calling black men to personal responsibility for problems that are largely not of their own making is confusing and harmful. The call for personal responsibility, without regard for its social contexts, can indeed be a way of letting off easy the society in which black men perish. For the most part, the march's organizers certainly downplayed the structural features of black male suffering. By linking morality to the personal, and not to the political as well, the march's organizers overlooked crucial social dimensions to black male problems. In some ways, the demand for atonement exaggerated black male responsibility by overestimating black male control. Plus, it gave solace to many on the right who had always said that personal responsibility was the cause, and, ultimately, the cure, for the problems black males face.

None of this means that we should ditch personal responsibility. It just means we've got to come up with a more complex version of responsibility, which remains an important element in rehabilitating black men's lives. Without an acknowledgment of moral agency, the black male becomes the sum of the social forces that shape him. Such a construction denies the moral capabilities of individual black men. It also underestimates the capacity for black men to change themselves and their communities. Feminists and other progressives who ignore personal responsibility deny the efforts of black men to behave humanely, especially toward black women and each other. It is true that a narrow conception of personal responsibility is harmful. It is equally true that a failure to appreciate the moral dimensions of social transformation is destructive. The conservatives aren't, and shouldn't be, the only ones concerned about responsibility.

To be fair, many black feminists supported the march. They didn't mind black men taking as much responsibility as they should for their actions. And that acceptance of responsibility didn't stop these feminists from believing that both white supremacy and black patriarchy have hurt black communities. The two beliefs aren't mutually exclusive. For these feminists, it was crucial for black men to understand the relationship between personal and collective responsibility. Admittedly, the call for responsibility was not as heavily politicized as I and others might have liked. And perhaps the march's organizers didn't have a sophisticated plan or vision to realize their moral aims. But their central aim, to help black men claim significant responsibility for themselves, was clear and cogent.

But other dimensions of the call to responsibility for black men were offensive. For instance, Farrakhan, and many of the men, failed to overcome their homophobia. The conservative view of the family held by the Nation, and by many blacks, devalues the role of gay men (and lesbian women) in the history of black struggle. That conservatism also discounts the intellectual contribution that gays and lesbians have made to the political and social health of black communities. Homophobia creates a form of intraracial apartheid. It was completely overlooked at the march, as a crude, simplistic view of racial unity prevailed. Similarly, the message of atonement, despite Farrakhan's oddly disjointed and esoteric oration on the subject, fell short of one of its most publicized aims: to communicate the failure of black men to treat black women right. There was nothing at the march to help black men atone for their misogyny, sexism, or patriarchy. These plagues have ripped through our communities, including our churches and our mosques.

I didn't expect Farrakhan to carry out this necessary housecleaning. I did, however, expect other speakers to make these points. The appearance of female speakers like Dorothy Height, Maya Angelou, and Betty Shabazz was especially troubling. Their presence compromised what for me was a key to the march: an all-male affair where we reckoned with how we had messed things up. Even more painful, these great women became pawns and tokens. It wasn't hard to figure out that these women weren't going to press black men about our failures in relating justly to black women. They weren't going to give feminist criticisms of patriarchy or homophobia. They weren't even going to speak about how some black men neglect or abuse their children. They did what they were expected to do: cheerlead. If these women were invited, then *all* women should have been invited. And represented. Making black women tokens and pawns at the march only confirmed the fears of some black feminists that black women aren't taken seriously, especially by the black men they often love and defend.

The charge of anti-Semitism against Farrakhan, too, plagued the march. It is a charge that has dogged Farrakhan as long as he has enjoyed the limelight as a militant black leader. The disdain many Jews feel for Farrakhan and Farrakhan's heroic status among many blacks, in part for his sharp criticism of Jews, are symptoms of the hostility and confusion that thwart peace between the two groups. A lot of the tension between blacks and Jews centers in issues of cultural assimilation and class ascension. Jewish assimilation was largely aided by the ease, and eagerness, of many Jews to blend, physically and psychically, into the white mainstream. Black assimilation has been slowed by the inability to blend. Since we live in a culture where social goods and benefits are attached to color, Jews and blacks embody opposing features of our society's obsession with skin: *pigmentification* and *pigmentosis*. Pigmentification occurs when white-skinned outsiders like Jews are adapted into the dominant culture, extending the benefits of democracy. Pigmentosis occurs when dark-skinned outsiders like blacks are excluded from the dominant culture, curtailing the benefits of democracy. The tension generated by Jewish identification with the white majority, and the exclusion of blacks from that possibility, continues to plague relations between the groups to this day.

The ascension of American Jews into the upper and ruling classes—aided by the amassing of Jewish wealth, prestige, and status, and the development of crucial Jewish networks of social, cultural, and political influence—has made the traditional liberal Jewish establishment less inclined to identify with poor, racially oppressed blacks.

Furthermore, the rise of conservative Jewish scholars who have delivered devastating, sometimes racist, criticisms of black culture has only deepened black hostility toward Jewish affluence and influence, while anti-Semitism from scholars such as Leonard Jeffries has infuriated Jews. The tension between Israel and her Islamic neighbors has been a source of tension with the Nation of Islam. Since quotas had been used to deny them educational and employment opportunities, many Jews opposed programs designed to redress racial inequality like affirmative action. Further, because of their experience in overcoming hardship, many Jews believed that once legal barriers to racism were removed, blacks should stop complaining and take advantage of the opportunity to succeed. These Jews failed to appreciate the persistence of informal racism. They also failed to appreciate the damaging effects of the folklore of racism, except, of course, when they shared in that folklore themselves. *Schwartze* was just as frequently uttered among Jews as kike was among blacks.

Although Farrakhan had been vilified by Jews for at least a decade—he had called Judaism a "gutter religion" during Jesse Jackson's 1984 presidential campaign—he was even more widely attacked because of the Nation of Islam's infamous 1991 publication, *The Secret Relationship Between Blacks and Jews. Secret* purports to show through the heavy use of Jewish scholarship, how deeply involved Jews were in the slave trade, and how Jews continue to exploit black Americans. *Secret* was a horrible piece of scholarship and a prejudiced view of Jewish culture. It is tragic that the Nation of Islam covers its anti-Semitism in the robes of scholarly objectivity, a ruse perfected by white racists like William Shockley and Arthur Jensen. Furthermore, the Nation implicitly asks those outside its ranks to discount the history of bias toward Jews in examining the Nation's harsh and bigoted beliefs about Jewish people and culture.

Legitimate, mutual criticism between blacks and Jews is distorted by extremists on both sides. When Jewish racism is cloaked in sophisticated intellectual jargon, it is nonetheless destructive. And when black anti-Semitism is given a smooth gloss because of its mixture of half-truth and falsehood, it is nonetheless harmful. Blacks and Jews cannot protect themselves from serious scrutiny behind cries of racism and anti-Semitism. For the most part, Farrakhan and his NOI acolytes, especially Khalid Abdul Muhammad, have angrily reduced legitimate disagreements with Jews to ethnic epithets and anti-Semitic sentiment. The Nation's obsession with Jews, the need to discover a Jew behind every problem that blacks face, informs their rhetorical assaults on Jews. Blacks and Jews must appeal to our humanist and religious traditions that promote the democratic exchange of ideas and grievances without resorting to vicious name-calling or immoral behavior.

Blaming Jews, gays and lesbians, and feminists, though it assuages our hurt in the short term, leads us down a moral spiral that favors self-pity at the expense of true self-examination and social change. The fact that the Million Man March promoted self-examination through the idea of atonement was the reason I signed on. Despite its problematic aspects, the march, and the masculine communion it encouraged, embodied some very important, healthy sentiments. Surely in the great variety of black men gathered on the mall, there were no unanimous views on political issues or on the precise definition of manhood. Some undoubtedly were still committed to homophobic, distorted notions of masculinity. But for others, there was a healthy assumption of responsibility.

Although the march marked a day of communion, there was a message to the larger society as well. The sheer presence of more than a million black men gathered peacefully to bear witness to their sorrows and successes was overwhelming. It symbolically repudiated stereotypes about black males. That they are mostly violent. That they can never get along. That they hate one another. That most of them are thugs or self-styled apologists for criminal behavior. That they lack values. That they have no interest in spiritual and moral matters. That they only blame social structures and blind forces for their problems.

As I see it, the Million Man March was an attempt by black men to publicly own up to our shortcomings. We have hurt black women and children through neglect, abuse, and indifference. The Million Man March was to have been a public ritual of accountability by black men for a shameful history of harm to our wives, sisters, mothers, sons, and daughters. This gesture of moral maturity didn't underplay the impact of white racism, as some critics claimed. It simply allowed black men to fess up to what our roles have been. In this case, making it an all-men's affair should have been an attempt from within to dismantle, not consolidate, male privilege. In my view, the Million Man March had the potential to inspire black men to embrace vulnerability as a mark of genuine masculinity, tenderness as a sign of our willingness to care.

SOLVING THE PROBLEMS OF BLACK MEN is but one element of coming to grips with the colossal problems that black folk confront. Of course, the much ballyhooed crisis of black leadership continues to seize the attention of black communities across America. Powell's emergence as a key figure in American politics continues to bolster the appeal of leadership that transcends race. In the end, the race transcendence that Powell symbolizes cannot successfully address the lethal persistence of race in our culture. The variety of ways that race, and racism, continue to dominate American culture will not be well served by a leadership whose success is pitted on suppressing key features of our racial malaise. Powell is right to focus on self-help, or raising by the bootstraps, as a prominent feature of black rehabilitation. But that's nothing new. Self-help has often been the only help black folk have known. But Powell also understands that you've got to have a good pair of boots to lift yourself up. Powell's vision of race transcendence is long on moral reconstruction, which is good. But it is short on social and cultural reconstruction. His vision of race transcendence fails to confront the structural features of American life that continue to harm black life. To take those factors seriously—factors like the maldistribution of wealth, the blight of capitalism, the material suffering of the impoverished, and class inequalities—is to challenge the deep conservatism of his political vision of the transcendence of race.

But neither will the race translation model of Farrakhan serve the best interests of black communities. Farrakhan is absolutely right to point out the continuing plague of white racism. He is right to accent personal responsibility. He is brave to preach to a spiritually hungry black America a message of moral and spiritual reconstruction. He is bold to articulate the forms of black rage that attract large segments of the black middle class. Farrakhan's appeal to the black middle class depends on the recognition that racism is not destroyed through higher class location or enhanced social status. The rage of the black middle class—a subject that journalist Ellis Cose has brilliantly explored—makes them, perhaps, the most surprising constituency of Farrakhan's expanded leadership. (In Malcolm's day, the black poor and working class were drawn to his message. Now, with a full generation of mainstream access, the black middle class has rediscovered the need to deal with the sheer recalcitrance of racism in America. Farrakhan is deeply attractive because that theme, along with the redemption of black men, is his bread and butter.)

Then too, the renewed appeal of Farrakhan—and Powell—to the black middle class is precisely because of black middle class guilt and anxiety toward the black ghetto poor. There is a lingering sense among the black (and white) middle class that Farrakhan is "good for those ghetto people." The support of Farrakhan's social conservatism is, in many ways, a cop-out for the black middle class. (Praising his leadership for the black ghetto poor is a little like praising Mussolini because he made the trains work on time.) All of this suggests that we need not only "bold leadership," but leadership that will allow for creative political alliances.

Still, Farrakhan's fundamentalist religious orientation—one that continues to express a vicious homophobia and a thinly veiled sexism—limits his use to progressive black forces confronting the racial challenges of the next century. Moreover, the ethnic bigotry that flows from Farrakhan's forces undermines their ethical integrity in pointing out the evil of white supremacy. Farrakhan's brilliant but narrow translation of race fails to account for the nuances, the robust diversity, the rugged complexity, the multihued textures of black life in America. If black folk are to move into the next century with serious, committed, well-equipped leadership, we need to be able to call our leaders to accountability for their actions. The antidemocratic nature of Farrakhan's religious organization makes that a difficult task. Farrakhan's appeal proves we need bold, visionary black leadership. But despite its virtues, a race translation model of black leadership fails to express the broad array of interests contained in the grammar of black liberation and resistance.

(Some may wonder, then, why I signed on to the Million Man March with Farrakhan at the helm. For the same reason that I: continue to teach at a white university that is often racist; preach in a black church that is often sexist and homophobic; lecture to groups that are often classist. Because we can't give up on ourselves. If we refused to participate in organizations because they're racist, bigoted, sexist, homophobic, classist, and misogynist, we'd have to stop participating in most synagogues, mosques, churches, schools, corporations, fraternities, and families! I have strong disagreements with Farrakhan, but where we can agree and use that agreement to build better communities, I have a moral obligation to work with him. And criticize him, as I've done here. As to the oft-made comparison between Farrakhan and white supremacist David Duke, that's easy. Duke operates out of a tradition that has hung, raped, murdered, maimed, injured, terrorized, and otherwise harmed black communities. It is a tradition of white supremacy. Farrakhan operates from a tradition of separatist black nationalist response to white supremacy. As offensive as I find aspects of Farrakhan's ideology, that tradition has not, generally speaking, done harm to anybody except, unfortunately, a few black folk.)

What we need is a black leadership that neither attempts to transcend nor translate race. We need a black leadership that *transforms* race. Race is transformed in this model of leadership because it joins a compelling account of what race has been to an articulation of what race can and should be. A race transforming black leadership is able to do at least three things. It accents the persistence of white supremacy. It challenges black orthodoxies about racial struggle on the left and right. And it links antiracist struggle to other forms of political resistance, including class and gender struggle.

Speaking about race, especially about the realities of white supremacy, is never easy. But in our age, it has become even more unpopular to do so. Public figures who call attention to the structural, moral, psychological, social, and cultural factors that preserve white supremacy are not tolerated for long. They are attacked as being politically correct. They are viewed as *ethnosaurs*, figures who can't let go of race as an explanation of the forces that hurt our nation. Or they are viewed as part of the very problem to which they call attention, just by virtue of pointing out the ugly obvious. But a race transforming leadership must hold up the mirror of cultural self-reflection so that the ugly obvious can be acknowledged and acted on. If they fail to highlight the historical contexts of white supremacy, race transforming leaders fail to help us move beyond mere finger-pointing or cathartic rage.

Next, race transforming black leadership challenges black orthodoxies on both ends of the ideological spectrum. The point here is not to occupy a neutral, middle ground. Race transforming leadership is decidedly committed to moving in a progressive, radical direction. The problem is that black folk are often reluctant to admit the limitations of perspective that hamper real transformation. So, for instance, the left's reluctance to talk about issues of virtues and values must be criticized. Just because we figure out that the right has got it wrong doesn't mean we shouldn't try to get it right. Broad segments of black communities are starving for moral engagement, spiritual rebirth, and ethical revival.

That's why Farrakhan is so appealing to many black folk. We are virtually ashamed to talk about such matters because they seem, well, unenlightened and almost primitive. They are not. Race transforming black leadership must highlight the role of moral and spiritual values in the social reconstruction of American life. It must demand attention to the habits, skills, and dispositions that lead to good behavior and sound judgment in black communities. Then, too, race transforming leadership must be willing to denounce the ill-conceived attacks on black communities launched by conservatives who have little concern for the suffering of persistently poor and working-class blacks. Race transforming black leaders must also be willing to challenge the sexual, gender, and moral conservatism of most black communities by linking historic forms of black struggles for liberation to the struggles of blacks who are gay, lesbian, feminist, and the like.

Finally, race transforming black leaders should be able to acknowledge the *centrality* of race while denying the *exclusivity* of race. Race transforming leadership should always keep its eyes on the effects of race, but it must never lose track of how race is shaped, distorted, configured, and conditioned by factors like class, gender, and sexuality. That means that race transforming leaders must forge links with other people and groups who are oppressed, besieged, attacked, undervalued, or marginalized in our culture. Of course, these coalitions will be hard to sustain. But such connections must be made. Black folk have been done in by a narrow vision of race loyalty already. Remember Clarence Thomas and Anita Hill? Race transforming leaders are able to see beyond the horizon of race as the only element making a difference to black folk. Thus, the class divisions within black life are not overlooked. Rich black folk are not the same as poor black folk. We are positioned differently in American culture, with different resources to combat our suffering. We even have different resources to be able to name what ails us.

The most powerful example of race transforming leadership in our time is Jesse Jackson. Jackson has worn several hats in defining a race transforming leadership: student protester, country preacher, civil rights worker, black nationalist firebrand, human rights activist, prophetic witness, moral advocate, social critic, public intellectual, political participant, presidential candidate, grassroots leader, and, above all, public moralist. Jackson has been extraordinarily consistent in his vocation of bearing witness to the suffering of, first, black folk, and increasingly, of migrant workers, farmers, gays and lesbians, environmentalists, feminists, and a host of "the least of these." Jackson's training in the arts of spiritual resistance and moral witness has shaped the core of his prophetic vocation. Like his mentor, Martin Luther King, Jr., Jackson is concerned about linking justice, power, and love. And King's martyrdom made it possible for Jackson to apply those principles to an arena of concern that King didn't live long enough to embrace: electoral politics. Jackson's presidential bids have forever changed the landscape of late twentieth-century American politics.

But more than that, Jackson has been out front on unpopular issues all along. He advocated black moral responsibility in black communities when Colin Powell was an Army comer and when Louis Farrakhan was fading on the vine of a small mosque on the west side of Chicago. He preached against black-on-black homicide before it became a widely discussed issue. Jackson preached tough love for black teens, in regard to both their sexual habits and their educational excellence. But Jackson, unlike most who share

191

his conservative cultural values, never lost sight of the structural realities, and the psychic deterrences, that prevented black folk from feeling like they were somebody. Jackson has proved a master on the stage of black psychic warfare and renewal. Perhaps that's because he fought so many early battles with the vicious denials of self-regard that his environment threw at him. In overcoming those odds, Jackson shaped his determination to succeed into a credo of self-affirming bravado that has left lesser souls in his dust.

To be sure, Jackson is not perfect. His organizations need to be more democratically ordered. And they should be given an institutional stability beyond the genius of his personality. Jackson is also often faulted for what some say is his lack of focus. That he's confronting Nike corporation one day, baseball owners the next day, working for migrant workers that night, for high school children the next morning, protesting against the Academy Awards that evening, and on and on and on. But whether or not that is a sign of Jackson's lack of focus, it is at least a sign of his outsized intellectual and moral ambition to link what appear to be disparate, discrete spheres of life into a coherent story of social transformation. Sure, at times Jackson's approach is scattershot. But his vision, and his needs and wants, are always great, even if his strategies to achieve his goals are sometimes weak and ill-conceived. His instincts, for justice, for the publicity that best serves his cause, and, yes, for his own interests, are usually right on the mark.

Jackson has been recently overshadowed by the bright light of Powell's emergence and Farrakhan's rise. But Jackson has been at this a lot longer than either of these two leaders. He is an Emersonian figure, an American original who has a knack for reinventing himself as the need arises. Jackson's leadership draws from the strengths of race transcendence and race translation. Like Powell, Jackson has ranged far beyond narrow black interests in articulating an ecumenical vision of social change. But unlike Powell, Jackson has remained rooted in a blackness that feels no need to suppress its particularity. Jackson has never believed that blackness was not itself a universally appealing identity. Jackson understands that blackness has gathered into its own formation a wonderful variety of social and cultural elements that make it eclectic and ever evolving. He knows that blackness is universal because it is hybrid: the combination of African and American roots.

Like Farrakhan, Jackson has consistently—even when it was unpopular to do so—talked about the wages of white supremacy. His vocation of prophetic witness has always realized the bitter persistence of race. As a public moralist Jackson has spoken to that persistence with edifying eloquence. Jackson has never forgotten the severe limits imposed on black folk for no other reason than that they were black folk. But unlike Farrakhan, Jackson has not allowed that understanding to thwart his embrace of every stripe and hue of American in figuring out how to overcome the lethal limitations of race. Jackson has worked hard to make sure that our social fabric does not unravel because of the punctures of racist thinking or behavior. Unlike Farrakhan, Jackson has taken the risk of broad political involvement. I'm not simply talking about politics in the electoral sense. I'm speaking of politics as the moral argument and action geared toward redefining the just possibilities of our social contract. Jackson understands that that sort of politics is achieved by our willingness to see beyond the horizon of selfish interest or bitter bigotries. Jackson has linked arms with people of every ethnic, racial, sexual, religious, and class background to make Martin Luther King, Jr.'s ideal of the beloved community a reality in our nation. In the long run, despite the brilliance of Powell and Farrakhan, this era in black social and political history will be known, because it has been shaped by the range of his success and the limits of his failure, as the Age of Jackson.

And we must be open to new race transforming black leaders as we approach the next century. For example, Laura W. Murphy is an ingenious young public intellectual, civil liberties advocate, and political activist who has worked tirelessly to protect the rights of racial and political minorities. As the first woman director of the American Civil Liberties Union's Washington Office, Murphy has been instrumental in getting landmark legislation passed, including the Family Medical Leave Act. Lisa Sullivan is a gifted grassroots organizer and a Field Director for the Children's Defense Fund. Sullivan has worked tirelessly with CDF founder and visionary Marian Wright Edelman to bridge the gulf between older and younger black generations, and to shine a light on the economic, social, and cultural problems affecting our nation's youth.

Constance Rice is a charismatic young black lawyer who heads the West Coast office of the NAACP Legal Defense and Educational Fund. Rice is a brilliant tactician, spellbinding orator, and legal wizard who has mobilized grassroots organizations and high-powered feminist groups to defeat the infamous California Civil Rights Initiative. And Monifa Akinwole is a 24-year-old New York talk radio host and national coordinator of the Malcolm X Grassroots Movement (MXG), which espouses black self-determination, human rights, and an end to sexist oppression. Akinwole has spearheaded the group's social activism, leading a boycott of Shell Oil because of its pollution of Nigeria's environment.

Still, black folk have missed out on other race transforming leaders because we have often looked simply to black male leadership. All the while, powerful, brilliant, insightful, demanding, cantankerous, sacrificial black women have been providing analysis, action, and answers. Women like Harriet Tubman, Sojourner Truth, Zora Neale Hurston, Mary McLeod Bethune, Pauli Murray, Fannie Lou Hamer, Ella Baker, JoAnn Robinson, Shirley Chisholm, Angela Davis, Jocelyn Elders, and on and on. It is the refusal to acknowledge the achievements of our black women that has, in great measure, hampered our progress as a race. Our ears must be opened. Their voices must be heard.

SIX

Behind Every Great Black Woman, There Are a Hundred More

Why Black Men Should Lighten Up

> *Nor am I referring here to the larger meta-phor of women, in the general commonweal of American life, as reflected by the statement: Behind every successful man stands a woman. Here I am talking about the force and energy of African-American women who, amid the general oppression of their gender, were always in the forefront of our inner struggle and ago-nies of the culture; always outnumbering the men on the hidden, but real, second and third lines of guidance and direction. They were pow-erful to us as a people for our nourishment and regeneration.*

> Leon Forrest
> "Spiritual Flight of Female Fire," 1991

IT WAS ONE OF THE MOST PAINFUL MEETINGS I have ever had to attend. It shouldn't have been. In fact, it should have been a time of great joy. After all, gathered here were women—strong, brilliant, sacrificial, progressive, no-nonsense, courageous, beautiful black women—whom I greatly admired. Every one of them. There were leaders I had been inspired by, like Jewell Jackson McCabe. There were intellectuals I had learned a great deal from, like Wahneema Lubiano, Gina Dent, Barbara Ransby, and Kimberle Crenshaw. There were writers whose work I had read and been taught by for years, like Marcia Gillespie. And there were women that I even, I must confess, idolized. Paula Giddings. Angela Davis.

Then why was this meeting so hard? Because I had gone there in part to join a group of black leaders, intellectuals, activists, and feminists who had opposed the Million Man March. But I'd gone to explain to these women—and one other black man—why I, an avowed feminist and progressive black intellectual, had attended the Million Man March. Had even, in my own small way, given it intellectual legitimacy, since I'd been public about my support of the march on several national television programs. (In fact, I'd appeared with Jewell Jackson McCabe and Glen Loury on one show, and with Kimberle Crenshaw and Randall Kennedy on another, to debate the meaning of the march.)

I already knew that Paula Giddings, a dear friend, was smoking mad at me. I'd been on the telephone with her, and on the receiving end of a blistering bawling out about my utter, well, stupidity, and my complicity in a shameless affront to the principles I claimed to live by. I was shaken, not just in the usual sense of being disconcerted after a bit of bad news. I was profoundly, morally shaken. I trusted Paula's instincts about these matters. I tried desperately to reconcile my need to go to the march with the equally compelling argument she made about why my decision was dumb.

And now I was going to this meeting—attended by many women with whom I'd effortlessly identified in the past—as, by no means the Enemy, but yes, in a sense, the Traitor. It was because of my deep love and respect for them, and my trust in their basic humanity—God, can't we, haven't we always depended on most black women for that?—more than my own decency or bravery, that I felt I could even face these sisters in struggle.

The gathering turned out to be as painful as I'd thought it would be. Like everyone in the room, I spoke my piece. I explained my reasons for going to the march. I talked of my brother, my son, my sense of desperation, my need for something serious to be done about the suffering and pain of black men. I confessed that I'd been disappointed by the tokenization of black women, the calculating way they'd been made into pawns. I explained that I was scheduled to speak—to launch a self-critical examination of black masculinity, how it needed redemption, yes, but also needed accountability to black women—but that I, and a few other speakers, didn't get a chance to have our say. I admitted that I felt ambiguous about the march now, precisely because it failed to make plain how black men should commit themselves to the work of getting rid of the bad habits that hurt black families. And I confessed as well that the reason I went in the first place was that black intellectuals tend to talk a lot, pontificate a lot, but not do anything. And to paraphrase Karl Marx, the point isn't to just think anymore, but to do something concrete and lasting.

Even more important than what I had to say was what the women had to say. How the march reinforced old stereotypes of black women. How it sharpened lines of division between "good" and "bad" women. How it assigned more weight to the pain and perspectives of black men. They spoke of the need for black men and black women to work, think, act, and resist together in the name of the principles of freedom to which we had all committed our lives. And they spoke of the need to continue to press a progressive, feminist analysis of our social and moral problems, even if against the stream or the temper of the times. They said that and a lot more.

As I listened, I became painfully aware, for the umpteenth time, of how messy, how maddeningly complex, are the relations between black men and black women. Why is it so difficult for brothers to hear the suffering of black women, to acknowledge their hurts, to embrace them as co-sufferers in a world where black skin and black bodies have been under extraordinary attack? Why is it so difficult for brothers to heal, or at least help relieve, the bitter traumas of spirit and flesh that black women face, often at the end of a black man's hands or words? And why is it so difficult for sisters to see that because we live in a patriarchal society, black men represent a special challenge to white male power? That black male bodies come under attack for being symbols of a sexual threat to white men, and to the women and girls they claim to protect? Those questions, and many, many more, still define our relations to one another. Still determine the extent to which we can see—or fail to see— that our lives are tied together. That last point, that our problems intersect in all sorts of strange and complex ways, is one that Kimberlé Crenshaw has brilliantly made. That's why, in the final analysis, we have to work side by side, not on top of, or below, one another. And yet, how can we reconcile intersection with specificity of pain? With the kind of pain that, yes, only black women can know. With the kind of pain that only black men can know. How can we make intersection and specificity work for us, use them as tools to uncover our common quest for humanity?

I SAW A DIFFERENT SIDE OF THIS PROBLEM when I had to go to another meeting. This one was decidedly more upbeat, but, in its own way, no less serious for the issues it raised. I was thrilled to be invited to appear on *Oprah* again. I was especially delighted this time because I was booked to give a male perspective on the sensation surrounding the film *Waiting to Exhale. Oprah* was always fun. Plus, I'd seen and enjoyed the show she'd done just a few weeks before with all the stars from the film. I thought it was about time black women got at least some of their due. I suspected there'd be a little sparring going on between the guests. After all, that's the setup of most talk shows.

But I certainly wasn't prepared for the opinions expressed by one of the other black male guests. He encouraged Americans to protest the film, claiming that it was insulting to black men. Of course, this wasn't a new argument. In fact, it was the same old tired argument many black men have been making for years. They made it when Toni Morrison began to publish. They made it when Alice Walker began to publish. Many black men certainly complained when Ntozake Shange began to write. And they plumb went off on Michele Wallace when her first book skewered cultural stereotypes of black men and women.

Now, I suppose, it was Terry McMillan's turn. When her novel *Waiting to Exhale* was published, it created a sensation. Here were four black women with man troubles. But in bonding they found a form of female companionship that helped them get through the tough times. When the movie was released in 1995, the tongues of black men started wagging again. Many complained that black men were taking a drubbing. That sisters needed to give brothers a break. I think it's mostly rubbish. Listen, I'm sensitive to the plight of black men. I've discussed it in every book I've written. But I think we've reached a limit with a particular kind of black male complaint. Especially when it's directed against the very black women who love and support black men.

To be sure, there are real tensions between black men and black women that need to be dealt with forthrightly. But the bellyaching of immature, self-doting, and self-pitying black men has got to stop. It takes away from serious matters. Matters that made a million men march. Matters that cause black women to be angry. This type of tired black male complaint was epitomized in the views of the other black male guest on *Oprah* that day. Among the many ludicrous things he said—and he was intelligent, not a crank by any means—the silliest was that the film *Waiting to Exhale* should be boycotted. Why? Because it destroyed the images of black men. He then made an absolutely ridiculous comment, comparing *Waiting to Exhale* to Hitler's hateful, spooky, and paranoid memoir, *Mein Kampf.* Enough is enough. Black men, we've got to grow up and get a life, maybe even several of them.

Black women deserve whatever good things happen to them. It doesn't diminish us as men for black women to receive a little of the limelight. Plus, half the time, sisters aren't even "studyin'" us. And when they are, they aren't being petty about black men the way black men are about black women. (Well, at least not most of the time.) As the response to the film suggests, black women simply want to see themselves through their own eyes. Not as the appendage of a man. Not as a bitch or a ho. Just beautiful, hardworking, striving women trying to make ends meet while balancing career, love, and self-discovery. Yeah, it's that simple.

Like the lusty Terry McMillan novel it's based on, *Waiting to Exhale* explores the joys and heartbreaks that dog women hungry for love. Contrary to all the black male complaint and controversy, all black men are not "bashed" at the hands of the film's female characters, even if the men turn out to be wrong for these women. (There's a difference, after all, between a film claiming that all men are dogs and that all the men in the film are dogs.) *Exhale* calls attention to the silly mistakes women make in their hunger for companionship. The film isn't about how terrible the guys are. (Can't you hear the refrain of the Carly Simon song, updated for our purposes: "You're so vain, I bet you think this film is about you"?) It's more about how sisters must be responsible for their own happiness.

The film's clear message is that women should honor their desire for intimacy. But they should also tame the desperation for love that turns them into fools or finger-pointers. The film insists that women should take charge of their lives. That's better than unhealthy coping strategies where women surrender themselves, body and soul, to their men. *Exhale*'s female characters learn to overcome harmful habits, like self-pity and self-debasement (a lesson brothers could use, too). They embrace self-examination and self-affirmation. Also, the women learn to love and support one another. Okay, the film may not have deep, profound feminist meaning. At least not on its high-gloss, black bourgeois surface. But it accents the beauty and value of female friendship. The bonds of mutual nurture between women depicted in the film can transform ties of intimacy into the makings of a vital, feminist community. You've got to meet people where they are to take them where they need to be.

I think *Exhale* shows that a network of female friendships, no matter how small, can help save women's lives. The main characters partly achieve this through the dying art of honest conversation. They confront the ugliness of their lives. They name the hidden forces that drive them to seek solace in men's arms before they search for it in self-reflection. Their poor choices of men have a lot to do with the women's lack of understanding about themselves. About their own needs. About their own desires. About their own interests. That lack of self-awareness turns out to be more decisive in the women's relationships than the men's inherent flaws. *Exhale* is more interested in highlighting the tortured female psyche, it's more concerned with how women can help one another regain their balance, than in pinpointing the wretched irresponsibility of *some* black men.

True enough, the males mostly take their lumps in *Exhale*. But the bruising that men endure is nothing when compared with the shameful, stereotypical treatment black women come in for in recent films directed by black men. Think of Janet Jackson's dismally drawn part as girl-in-the-hood "Justice" in John Singleton's *Poetic Justice,* the uninspired and uninspiring follow-up to his brilliant debut, *Boyz N The Hood.* And let's not forget Spike Lee's cardboard female leads in *School Daze,* including Tisha Campbell's turn as a shallow, high-class "ho." (For that matter, many black male parts in films directed by black men are either underdeveloped or exaggerated.) Besides, *Exhale* was intelligently directed by Forrest Whitaker, a black man. And the film's superb soundtrack was orchestrated by Babyface, a black man. Those are big clues that black women seem more willing than black men to share power and perspective with the opposite sex.

Exhale humorously and skillfully undresses the myth of black male sexual superiority. On the surface, that's a painful gesture. It kicks the props from underneath the last symbol of cultural dominance—besides dominance in sports—that black men seem to enjoy. But destroying that myth can free black men from the prison of sexual performance (not that many inmates want to be set free!). It might encourage us to pay more attention to the delicate and demanding art of making love. It may sound trite, even corny, but sweetness more than sweat is the measure of genuine intimacy.

To be sure, *Exhale* fails to help us navigate the difficult domain where sexual and social intimacy collide. The film barely touches on this serious problem in the relations between black men and women. How do black women help to protect one another from exploitative brothers even as they defend brothers from the ravages of white supremacy? That's no small matter. Maybe that's why the film steers clear of the subject. But it's got to be addressed. Of course, in such a problem we hear echoes of the Million Man March and the O.J. Simpson trial. Those issues inevitably bleed into the frames of the film, though the film doesn't help us to frame the issues with more clarity than we already have, or, in any case, lack. Surely those issues were reverberating in the minds of black viewers as they sat in theaters eating up their popcorn along with the beautiful beige beauty, the ebony eroticism, they saw on the screen.

In one sense, we pay the film a big compliment by asking too much of it. After all, it's only a film. It's even only one film. But since we've had such little serious treatment of the lives of black women, we overload the film with all our frustrations and fantasies. *Waiting to Exhale* is a landmark film. Not because of the pedigree of its achievement. It is a good, not a great, film. It's important because it realistically, lovingly, but not exhaustively, presents four trouble-in-love middle-class "sisters." They aren't martyrs. They aren't mammies. They aren't Jemimas. And they aren't Jezebels.

Sure, they are all beautiful, and romance—not just the erotic kind, but the one of image—is thick. But then, there are millions of middle-class black women who aren't represented in the bitch-of-the-week or ho-of-the-month flavors that continually spill from Hollywood or from rap songs. This film is just the tip of the iceberg. There are millions of real, but largely invisible, black women who saw themselves, or bits of themselves or their friends, in this film. Of course, now we're going to get another installment of black folk being in style for a season. There will be copycat films. But shouldn't the girls have their day? Maybe they'll get enough financing to draw broad, brilliant, searing portraits of black women that won't need to make a lot of money in order to be successful. If that happens, it will be because of the success of films like *Waiting to Exhale. Exhale*'s greatest contribution may be that it forces us to go home and think about some of the stupid stuff we do. And some of the crazy stuff we put up with. And why. Above all, it might just make us think about why too often black men and women who are in each other's beds are at each other's throats.

INDEED, THE ANTAGONISM BETWEEN black men and women is a subject that I hoped would be addressed with more skill and insight than we managed at the Million Man March. I realize that it is easier to talk about how black men and women should come together and love one another than it is to figure out how to do it. But there is a simple way for us to begin. We can become self-critical black men. If black men really want to be leaders, I think we should clarify our part in mending the wounding rifts between black men and women. Black men must address our failure to be the kind of black men that our communities demand, that our history has brought forth, that our futures depend on.

We needn't worry that by so doing we allow white folk to say "Aha, we told you black men were failures." Millions of white folk were heartened by the show of love, strength, and unity—and the desire to be responsible—by black men in the Million Man March. (Let's hope those same whites are equally committed to coming up with the financial, political, and moral resources needed to make sure that millions more black males have the chance to behave with dignity and self-assurance in the future.) And we don't have to fear that black women will see us as weak, or as somehow conceding that we have been the sole source of conflict between the sexes all along. Millions of black women are still hungry for black men who don't mistake violence for strength, tenderness for weakness, or sensitivity for sentimentality.

In short, self-critical black men can make a healthy difference in black communities. I became even more convinced of this truth when I attended the meeting with Angela Davis, Paula Giddings, and other heroic sisters. Their perspectives made me even sadder that I didn't get the opportunity to address the mighty mass of men assembled in Washington. I had written my speech, which I titled "Between Pain and Possibility," with self-critical black men in mind. I offer it now as a gesture of my willingness to speak about the problems black men face, and about the problems we've caused black women to endure. I hope it will help us to dialogue and make decisions about how black men and women can embrace one another as allies in the quest for liberation and wholeness.

As BLACK MEN, WE HAVE COME to this hallowed spot in our nation's history to extend the sacred pursuit of freedom and truth that binds our democracy together. As black men, we have come to test our country's resolve to make justice as crucial and as common as the air we breathe. As black men we have come to rescue a conversation about race and masculinity that is trapped between stereotype and romance.

Let us concede right away that this monumental show of solidarity is at once thrilling and threatening. Black men have so rarely been encouraged to assemble under our own lights—free of white patronage or paranoia—that the mere sight of thousands of brothers rising to boldly salute the best in us is frightening. For too long, a lethal legacy of distrust and self-hatred has suffocated the regard and affection that should travel freely between black men. Our mutual contempt bleeds in the cruel ingenuity we employ to snuff out one another's lives in word or deed. This gathering is a mighty rejection of black male death in every guise. It is a soaring affirmation of the redemptive potential of black men loving, and learning from, and listening to, one another.

This demonstration of strength and dignity also permits black men to confess our sins and to clarify our suffering. The signs of black male suffering, and our sins, are painfully apparent. U.S. prisons are packed with black bodies. Unemployment lines swell with black males. Infant mortality rates rise on the cushiony spines of black male babies. AIDS and homicide are the bitter prizes in a lottery of black male self-destruction. A staggering number of black teens drop out of high school each year. Criminal behavior corrupts thousands of youth. Racism incites police brutality of black males. Ignorance fuels the fear of black men, even among the well-educated, whose anger is a constant reminder of unfulfilled justice.

Yet, even as we list the litany of ills that befall black males, we must be mindful of the many plagues that mock the prosperity of black females. Single-female-headed households experience economic trauma. Teen mothers struggle under the weight of emotional and financial hardship. Black women have extraordinary incidents of breast and cervical cancer. Sexism and racism deliver a powerful one-two punch to the social aspirations of black women. The sexual and domestic abuse of black females continues to receive less attention than that of white women. And perhaps most painful of all, black men continually reinvent the wheel of patriarchy to trample the lives of black women.

Indeed, we cannot ignore how this march, for many of our sisters, mothers, daughters, and wives, is a brutal slap in the face. For many black women, this march is a graceless gesture of ingratitude for the constancy of companionship they have shown black men from the beginning of our time together on American soil. And no words I utter here today—no efforts at explanation or comfort that any of us can extend, really—will relieve many black women's anger and suspicion of our motives in marching.

That's because too often black men have tried to siphon off the bitter dregs of white patriarchy and recycle them to our families as the sweet wine of enlightened leadership. That's because too often black men have criticized white racism while ignoring the harmful, even violent, sexism and misogyny we endorse. That's because too often black men resent or abandon black women because we think they have it better in a white world that in reality taxes them three times over—for their gender, their race, and their economic situation. That's because too often black male talk about redeeming or healing black families is a poorly disguised attempt to subordinate black women and to unfairly discipline black children.

Unfortunately, rhetoric about restoring black male leadership in families is often joined to vicious homophobic beliefs that turn on purging the black family of queers and queens. In rap, and in religious circles, heterosexual black men have tried to exclude the pain and perspectives of gay males. Such bigoted practices trump our moral authority. They enlist black men in just the sort of campaign of intolerance we seek to oppose. It's clear from our condition—especially our problems with women, children, gays and lesbians, and each other—that black men's understanding of the pains and possibilities of black masculinity must be transformed.

But we cannot help transform ourselves with simplistic clichés and worn-out watchwords. There is a prophetic and poignant passage in the Bible that captures our predicament. In Jeremiah, the eighth chapter and twentieth verse, these haunting, beautiful, and sad words appear: "The harvest is past, the summer is ended, and we are not saved." For black men, the meaning of these words is clear. Many of the beliefs that we have embraced, and the passions that we have invested in those beliefs, have come to a dead end. They have no power to heal or redeem us.

This is not merely a compelling indictment of black men's refusal to reform ourselves. It also signals this nation's failure to honor its obligation to fix the mess it has created. We come to our nation's capital today to claim our share of moral responsibility for what we have made of our lives. But we also come to call our country to vigilance in exercising its responsibility to address the sexual, material, and racial ruin that rots the core of American democracy.

The harvest of our national and personal neglect is past, the summer of playing roulette with unsatisfying remedies is ended, and we are not saved.

The harvest of racism, patriarchy, and homophobia is past, and we are not saved.

The harvest of sexual abuse and domestic violence is past, and we are not saved.

The harvest of remaining indifferent to the economic suffering of poor black men is past, and we are not saved.

The harvest of misogyny in hip-hop, and in the mosque, the temple, the synagogue, the cathedral, and the church is past, and we are not saved.

The harvest of demonizing young black males as the embodiment of everything we find culturally reprehensible is past, and we are not saved.

The harvest of highlighting personal pathology and ignoring this nation's role in the structural and moral brutalities of the black ghetto is past, and we are not saved.

Black men can only be saved when we insist that our suffering is both within our hands and beyond our grasp. It is both personal and political, both individual and institutional.

Black men can only be saved when we recognize that in highlighting our specific pain, we must not obscure, distort, or deny the pain of black women and children.

Black men can only be saved when we realize that we shouldn't rule over our families, but cooperate with our partners to help guide our children.

Black men can only be saved when we pull off our macho costumes and make ourselves vulnerable to the discipline and rewards of self-examination.

Black men can only be saved when we reject homophobia and embrace all black men as our brothers in the struggle to redefine masculinity and to preserve our sanity.

Black men can only be saved when economic and moral transformation inspire us to give up guns and gangs, and the violence that too many of us believe to be both our birthright and our unfailing destiny.

Black men can only be saved when we surrender the physical and psychological advantage we have gained over women through abusive language and behavior.

Black men can only be saved when we help bring the ideals of radical democracy to sure realization for all who are poor and distressed.

Black men can only be saved when we use our suffering and struggle to forge connections with all who are victimized by the unrealized promise of the American dream, a dream to which Martin Luther King added brilliant color 32 years ago.

This march is a majestic reminder of black men's willingness to speak our pain and to imagine the possibilities of a brighter future. We have marched today, not to put anybody down, but to lift up the sorrows and successes of men whose stories are not often told in their rich diversity and complexity. We have marched today to feel the edifying power of black male unity. We have not marched to harm, but to embrace one another. We have not marched to fortify, but to dismantle, patriarchy.

We have marched to be better sons to our mothers. We have marched to be better husbands to our wives. We have marched to be stronger mates to our partners. We have marched to be better fathers to our daughters. We have marched to tell our sons that we love them. We have marched to tell our brothers that we need them. We have marched to tell our fathers that we admire them. We have marched to tell our uncles that we respect them. We have marched to tell our friends that we depend on them.

And we have marched to tell ourselves, and this nation, that we want to be real men. Real men don't attack their loved ones. Real men don't shirk their duties. Real men temper strength with wisdom and know how to share power. Real men aren't afraid of real women. And real men constantly fashion our behavior in the world to bring about justice and peace. Real men understand the grammatically broken but spiritually eloquent words of the old, black church mother who said: "Be who you is, and not who you ain't; 'cause if you is what you ain't, you am what you not." That's a motto that real men, and indeed all of us, should learn to live by.

In a Color-blind Society, We Can Only See Black and White

Why Race Will Continue to Rule

The rules may be color-blind, but people are not. The question remains, therefore, whether the law can truly exist apart from the color-conscious society in which it exists, as a skeleton devoid of flesh; or whether law is the embodiment of society, the reflection of a particular citizenry's arranged complexity of relations.

Patricia J. Williams
The Alchemy of Race and Rights, 1991

"MICHAEL ERIC DYSON...any sense of why these things are going on?" Charlie Gibson, the literate host of *Good Morning America,* asked me.

He was referring to the recent rash of burnings that have gutted nearly seventy black churches since January 1, 1995. In the brief time I had—shared with eloquent guests Deval Patrick, U.S. Assistant Attorney General for Civil Rights, and Morris Dees, Director of the Southern Poverty Law Center— I suggested two factors. First, black churches are vulnerable targets for white rage, especially since even rural churches symbolize black presence and progress. Second, the burnings are an outgrowth of our nation's lethal racial climate.

To be honest, no one can say for certain why black churches are being targeted for fiery destruction, mostly in the South. In the '60s black churches were the headquarters for those enlisted in the army of nonviolent resistance to state-sponsored apartheid. The church kitchen provided nourishment to famished troops, offices became war rooms to develop strategies, and sanctuaries became rallying posts where the charge to battle was sounded. In the perverse reasoning of white supremacists, it made sense to bomb and burn churches as a way to terrorize blacks, to discourage them from fighting for racial justice.

While the church remains at the center of black life in the '90s, it is now more venerable than threatening. In part, that's a reflection of how our times have evoked less dramatic demonstrations of the church's role in social transformation. In that light, it is curious that black churches—not the large, urban, affluent ones, but mostly modest, rural houses of worship—are once again being consumed by more than the Holy Spirit.

The fact that we can't get a good grip on what's going on, that we can't draw from these church burnings the clear conclusions that old-style racism made possible, is an ironic sign of progress. In the '60s and before, acts of hatred had symbolic clarity because blacks and whites shared an ecology of race. I'm not suggesting that blacks and whites agreed about what each group saw as the source of racial conflict. In fact, like today, they often didn't even agree about what they saw: many whites saw roses where many blacks saw thorns. Blacks and whites also bitterly disagreed about what they should do about the problems that existed. Still, the racial environment they inherited and shaped made the discerning of racist symbols easier. A church burning was undisguised racial hatred. A cross burning was meant to intimidate "uppity" blacks. And a lynching was the ultimate expression of a white supremacist desire to control the black body.

But in our more racially murky era—an era in which the ecology of race is much more complex and choked with half-discarded symbols and muddied signs—our skills of interpretation have to be more keen, our readings more nuanced. There's little doubt that most of the vitriolic expressions of racism have been forced underground by the success of '60s black freedom struggles. But symptoms of racial antipathy persist, even if they're harder to prove and far more difficult to analyze.

Our current racial climate, which encourages the belief that we do, or should, live in a color-blind society, has made many commentators wary of claiming a connection between the church burnings. Some commentators claim that these burnings are more religious than racial, since so many white churches have also been burned. Some commentators believe that claiming a connection between the burnings might give heart to isolated racists by exaggerating the degree to which a concerted effort to rattle black folk even exists among the perpetrators. In other words, these commentators seek to avoid claiming that a conspiracy to destroy black churches exists. Well, if not all racial meanings have been driven underground, some of them are hidden in plain sight. We miss them because they're right in front of our faces.

There are various reasons for some of the black church burnings: teenage vandalism, mental derangement, and, in a couple of cases, insurance fraud. (Though we should ask why a black church is viewed as a viable target for a disgruntled teen or a confused young adult.) Among those twelve arsonists already convicted of burning black churches in the '90s, however, there is a definite pattern of racial hostility. A couple of them felt they were being cheated at a black-owned juke joint in Tennessee, while another was angered that his daughter had run off with a black man. Torching a black church was a way to get revenge.

All twelve of the arsonists are white, and all of them were convicted under a 1965 federal civil rights law. Two other arsonists, both white, are in jail awaiting trial, as federal prosecutors prepare to charge them under civil rights law.

The twelve share other similarities. Ten didn't finish high school. Half were unemployed, while others were stuck in low-paying jobs. Ten are young, ranging in age from seventeen to twenty-three. Half lived at home with their parents, most in rural areas near the churches they burned. And three had explicit ties to racist groups.

The perpetrators' profiles make it clear that black churches symbolize to them—and perhaps to other arsonists as well—not the civil rights threat of old, but a local sign of black survival, of black success. The rural black church in particular captures the utility—it is a major outlet for social recreation—and the invincibility of black Christian faith. Ironically, those very qualities have made it newly vulnerable to another generation of confused, disgruntled, racist whites. We need not hunt for a Grand Conspiracy to explain what's going on. It would then be easy to scapegoat poor whites. Rather, our very racial ecology—littered with code words, hidden racial meanings, thinly veiled racial assumptions, and confused racial rules, while witnessing the emergence of racist militias and the resurgence of white hate groups—conspires against racial justice. Church burnings are merely the most obvious sign of a more dangerous racial fire raging in our nation.

To make matters worse, many of the guardians of our legal and political culture are busy retarding real racial progress by invoking the same principles of justice and equality for which blacks heroically fought and often died. One of the bitter ironies of this situation is that many of the former opponents of racial equality are now charged with dispensing racial justice in local, state, and federal governments. The fox who once terrorized the chicken coop is now expected to be fair to the chickens—to know best what they need, and to determine what measures are just in their pursuit of equality with the foxes.

That bitter irony is compounded by the fact that laws aimed at equality and justice are often interpreted by those who have done little of the suffering that brought the laws into existence. As a result, the spirit of struggle that helped make the laws a vibrant fulfillment of democracy is nullified. And the history of racial conflict that shaped how those laws should be understood and applied is obscured, distorted, or simply erased.

I'm certainly not arguing that one has to have been

victimized by slavery, a denial of rights after Reconstruction, or the rule of Jim Crow to interpret or apply laws meant to realize racial justice. That kind of petty identity politics is harmful to historically wronged blacks who are much larger and more complex than the labels of suffering they wear. Neither am I arguing that blacks should demonize those who disagree with us about how to bring about justice and equality. It's one thing to say let freedom ring. It's another matter to determine who gets to strike the liberty bell, when it should be rung, and what our responses should be to what we hear. Still, there's no denying that, in terms of racial politics, where you stand—and the history that makes that stance both possible and plausible—determines what you see and hear. If the Rodney King beating, and the riots that followed his molesters' acquittal, didn't make that clear, then the O.J. Simpson trial and its aftermath should leave little doubt that it's true.

THE MOST RECENT EXAMPLE of our tragic confusion about how racial justice should be conceived and applied is the 1996 Supreme Court decisions that ruled four congressional districts—one in North Carolina and three in Texas—unconstitutional. The Court invalidated the districts because race played a predominant role in their creation. The four districts had been created after the 1990 census to give minorities more just electoral representation. The Supreme Court's 5-4 rulings buttress three previous decisions in which the Court said race should not be the main reason for drawing odd-shaped districts that pull together minority voters to maximize their electoral strength. So while districts may be legally redrawn to protect political incumbents, they cannot be drawn to support previously and presently excluded minority voters.

What's tragic about the Court's decision is that it is based in large part on an ahistorical interpretation of the Fourteenth Amendment. We should recall that the Fourteenth Amendment was passed after the Civil War to extend to former slaves equal protection under the law. In his majority decision against the district (in the North Carolina case, *Shaw v. Hunt*), Chief Justice William Rehnquist argued that racial "classifications are antithetical to the Fourteenth Amendment, whose central purpose was to eliminate racial discrimination emanating from official sources in the States."

But what Rehnquist fails to address is how congressional districts drawn with race in mind are a response to the 1965 Voting Rights Act, passed to guarantee the right to vote for blacks who should already have been protected by the Fourteenth Amendment. If that amendment was insufficient to help enforce legal enfranchisement for blacks, it is ironic that the supposed failure to abide by it is now evoked by the Supreme Court to further erode electoral representation for those same blacks.

Before the 1990 census led to the creation of majority-minority districts, there were 26 black members in Congress. In 1992 that number rose to 39, and in 1994 there were 41 black members in Congress. In North Carolina, two majority-minority districts helped send the first two black North Carolina legislators to Congress since George White was forced out of Congress in 1901 by the state's ratification of a disfranchisement Amendment. In the words of white turn-of-the-century North Carolina Democratic leader Charles Aycock, the ratification of the disfranchisement amendment was "the final settlement of the negro problem." Unsurprisingly, Aycock was elected governor of North Carolina in the same election in 1901. When Congresswoman Eva Clayton, of North Carolina's first district, and Congressman Melvin Watt, of the twelfth district, took their seats in the House in 1993, the promise of the Fourteenth Amendment, reinforced by the Voting Rights Act of 1965, was at long last realized.

An even greater irony is that the Court ruled against the majority-minority districts because they failed to satisfy the Court's criteria, established in a 1993 ruling, that a "compelling state interest" be reflected in the drawing of the districts, and that the districts should be drawn in a way that was "narrowly tailored" to serve that interest. Certainly the proportional representation of black voters is a "compelling state interest." But Rehnquist wrote: "an effort to alleviate the effects of societal discrimination is not a compelling interest."

And according to Justice Sandra Day O'Connor's opinion for the majority in the Texas case, *Bush v. Vera,* more judicial weight is given to the geographical shape of a district than to its political utility in realizing the aims of the Fourteenth Amendment and the Voting Rights Act. "The bizarre shape and noncompactness demonstrated by the districts...cause constitutional harm insofar as they convey the message that political identity is, or should be, predominantly racial," O'Connor writes. With one stroke of her pen, O'Connor denies the role that race has historically played in shaping political identity. She also completely ignores how racial identity is politicized, since it doesn't exist in a protected zone outside our nation's profound political conflicts. One can only conclude that, at least when it comes to racial politics and majority-minority districts, Freud was right. Anatomy *is* destiny.

Of course, alternatives to district-based representation, and hence, to racial redistricting, have been put forth. Alas, they have gone the way of all political flesh, or at least such ideas have been castigated as "profoundly antidemocratic." Lani Guinier, for instance, suggested that geographically based constituencies deny individual representation of the voter. She has written that "the use of geographic districts as the basis for establishing representational constituencies is at its very heart a system of group-based representation."

What to do? Guinier suggested an alternative to the winner-take-all manner of our current single-member congressional districts. Instead, we might have multiseat congressional districts where each voter has several votes that can be distributed among many candidates. Or we might have preference voting, where voters rank their votes in order of preference. But Guinier's notions of cumulative and preference voting got her dubbed a "quota queen" in the *Wall Street Journal.* She was widely dismissed as a fringe radical whose ideas made her unfit for the Assistant Attorney General for Civil Rights post, for which her nomination was withdrawn by President Clinton in 1993. A year later, without any controversy, Supreme Court Justice Clarence Thomas, in an opinion for a voting rights case, wrote that in "principle, cumulative voting and other non-district-based methods of effecting proportional representation are simply more efficient and straightforward mechanisms for achieving what has already become our tacit objective: roughly proportional allocation of political power according to race."

It is clear from the Supreme Court's decisions about majority-minority districts and other recent decisions severely undermining the scope of affirmative action, and from the effect its decisions have had on black communities, that the Court is failing miserably as the guardian of racial justice. Justice O'Connor is worried that by creating majority-minority districts, we will forget that "voters are more than racial statistics." What she fails to understand is that without legal guarantees of equal protection and just representation, the interests of black voters will remain largely unrepresented. The Supreme Court's judgments underscore a dilemma the Court has failed to successfully address: how our nation can overcome racism without taking race into account.

The Supreme Court has consistently, at least recently, argued for the ideal of a color-blind society. Ironically, that ideal has led the Court, and other would-be advocates of black interests, to overlook the history of sacrifice, suffering, and struggle that made the Fourteenth Amendment and the Voting Rights Act necessary. (In fact, Robinson Everett, the Duke law professor who instigated the North Carolina suit, and who argued it before the Supreme Court, is a self-described "yellow dog Democrat" who believes in a color-blind politics inspired by 1960s social activism. Everett and other southern white Democrats are heartened by the Supreme Court ruling because it will spread blacks throughout districts where white politicians have a better chance of being elected, since blacks vote overwhelmingly Democratic. This is another instance where alleged black allies inflict the deepest wounds to black interests with the double-edged sword of political opportunism sharpened on either side by race.)

Over the last decade, the Supreme Court has consistently failed to appreciate the complexities of the history of race in America. As Justice John Paul Stevens writes in his dissenting opinion, it is unfortunate that the Court should intervene "into a process by which federal and state actors, both black and white, are jointly attempting to resolve difficult questions of politics and race that have long plagued

North Carolina." Stevens recognizes that the Court's ruling means, in effect, that all sorts of political interests can be legally protected save those that are based on race. Stevens doesn't "see how our constitutional tradition can countenance the suggestion that a State may draw unsightly lines to favor farmers or city dwellers, but not to create districts that benefit the very group whose history inspired the Amendment that the Voting Rights Act was designed to implement."

The disagreement about race in America's highest court reflects the fatal disagreements that continue to bewitch our nation. Those courageous black souls who fought to make America all that it should be were not interested in what is presently meant by a color-blind society. True enough, they were interested in shaping an American society that wasn't obsessed with race, that didn't use race to unfairly dispense goods or allocate resources. But most were not naive enough to believe that we could ever, in the foreseeable future, arrive at a place where race didn't make a huge difference in how we live our lives, how we view one another, how we are granted or denied social privilege.

The tragedy of our condition is that we have a Supreme Court, and many other Americans, who have ignored the rules of race, how race continues to shape American life. Worse yet, they blame those who resist the color-blind myth for extending, rather than exposing, the hold race still has on the American character. But we cannot overcome the history of racial oppression in our nation without understanding and addressing the subtle, subversive ways race continues to poison our lives. The ostrich approach of burying our collective head in the sands of historical amnesia or political denial will not work. We must face race head on.

The ideal of a color-blind society is a pale imitation of a greater, grander ideal: of living in a society where our color won't be denigrated, where our skin will be neither a badge for undue privilege nor a sign of social stigma. Because skin, race, and color have in the past been the basis for social inequality, they must play a role in righting the social wrongs on which our society has been built. We can't afford to be blind to color when extreme color consciousness continues to mold the fabric and form of our nation's history. Color consciousness is why black churches continue to burn. Color consciousness is why Supreme Court justices bend over backward to repress the memory and present manifestation of racial inequality.

But we can strive for a society where each receives his or her just due, where the past in all its glory and grief is part of the equation of racial justice and social equality. Then we won't need to be blind to color, which in any case is a most morbid state of existence. Then we can embrace our history and our ideals with the sort of humane balance that makes democracy more than a distant dream.

If You Is What You Ain't, You Am What You Not

Black English and Black Identity

Words' meanings, but also the rhythm and syntax that frame and propel their concatenation, seek their culture as the final reference for what they are describing of the world. . . . Being told to "speak proper," meaning that you become fluent with the jargon of power, is also a part of not "speaking proper." That is, the culture which desperately understands that it does not "speak proper," or is not fluent with the terms of social strength, also understands somewhere that its desire to gain such fluency is done at a terrifying risk. The bourgeois Negro accepts such risk as profit. But does close-ter *(in the context of "jes a close-ter, walk wi-thee") mean the same thing as* closer? *Close-ter, in the term of its user is, believe me, exact. It means a quality of existence, of actual physical disposition perhaps . . . in its manifestation as a tone and rhythm by which people live.*

Le Roi Jones
"Expressive Language," 1966

THE SONG BLARED OUT OF CAR RADIOS last spring like a twisted April Fool's joke, but for millions of blacks, it was a four-minute coon show that glorified ghetto stereotypes while exposing the deadly shamelessness of rap music.

"Who dat is?" the male voice demands.

"My baby's daddy," the female voice replies.

The rap is about the difficulties of living with a woman who makes suspicious claims that a host of male callers are her infant's father. For many blacks, it was bad enough that the song merely mimicked the hazards of intimacy, especially the paradox of keeping love fresh while keeping the same partner, without admitting that the desultory domesticity that passes for home life is one of the biggest hazards of all. Even worse for such critics, the rap refused to imagine the severe toll that teen love might exact on the body-and-soul of the child. If the subject matter was sordid, there was something even more troubling in the language. Because the song's refrain, which doubles as its title, is rapped in Black English, the link between bad grammar and deficiency—in this case, a moral, if not intellectual, one—is made painfully clear.

Indeed, the response of many blacks to "Who Dat Is" is a faint echo of the widespread outrage evoked by the recent "Ebonics" controversy. When the Oakland School Board voted to recognize Ebonics (coined in 1973 by Robert Williams, the term combines "ebony" and "phonics"), or Black English, as a separate language, black and white critics plumbed the same inkwell in a rare show of multiracial media disgust. There was near-universal agreement that Black English rests on an intellectually faulty premise. After all, hadn't glittering stones of black eloquence been hewn from a mountain of grammatical obstacles that Oakland now sought to place in the educational pathways of black children as a Mount Sinai of pedagogical salvation? The belief was widely held, too, that there was a moral taint to the Oakland School Board's decision: it was a scheme to win money and sympathy in the face of failure, it was a foolhardy plan to alchemize street talk into a gold mine of respectable speech.

Such a reaction was wholly expected from mainstream white media and culture. Black literacy developed against the backdrop of white resistance in slavery; America was hugely convinced of the revolutionary economic and political consequences of blacks learning to read and write English. As a result, our nation wrote the prohibition of black literacy into its laws. Then, too, America forbade the black slave the luxury of openly developing self-defending verbal arts; back talk, wisecrack remarks, spotting mistakes in white speech, rhetorical cleverness, and the like threatened the racial hierarchy and were brutally discouraged.

Still, blacks aimed for literacy in the slave quarter and worked diligently to piece together a language that reflected the propriety of self-expression and the priority of survival. Literacy provided blacks with an opportunity to reinvent themselves. The rhythms, idioms, semantics, syntax, grammar, dialects, vernaculars, and rhetorics of black language are crucial means by which blacks shape their social identities. A great virtue of black literacy is that it permits blacks to interpret their personal experience of race through a grand story of shared struggle for racial stability. In such a story— composed of the formal and the informal, the written and the oral, the sacred and the secular—black identity is protected against a harmful presumption of blackness as evil or incompetent. Black English is the syntax of black survival, the grammar of black aspirations to achieve self-definition in a white world that attempted to will it, to write it, into oblivion.

It is no surprise that many whites view Black English with a mixture of contempt, pity, and ignorance even as the white mainstream benefits from an unconscious absorption of black speech into American culture. When Black English is made a commodity in rap music, or when the lexicon of American hipsterism swells with black sayings, many white Americans understand, even value, parts of black speech. When Black English is pressed to serve the interests of white culture, or to entertain the white masses—like other areas of black culture that have been adapted, co-opted, appropriated—it is bleached to white perfection or left black enough so that it feels exotic, and in other cases, vulgar or violent.

But if Black English gives America a black eye, the favor is returned in a double portion of negativity as our nation bruises both the notion and the people who turn such loving eyes on themselves. When blacks attempt, through embracing Black English or supporting black colleges, to rescue themselves from the tragedy of being unloved or unknown, or to remedy the failure to love and know themselves, their efforts are often resisted. This is true even for well-meaning whites who are determined to help black folk by denying them, whether it's a seat in Congress, a spot in law school, a job in corporate America, or a pedagogy that meets kids where they are in order to take them where they need to be, such as what was proposed by the Oakland School Board. The white resistance to Black English was, in this light, unremarkable.

More remarkable, and utterly disheartening, however, was the hysteria of elite blacks that greeted the debate about Black English. Critics tried to outdo themselves in heaping invective on the Oakland School Board, without even attempting to understand what they were doing or why. Such responses might have been expected, and even understandable, in light of the coverage the mainstream white media gave the Ebonics debacle early on. It was framed as a ludicrous plot to teach black kids street slang in place of rigorous attention to written and rhetorical skills.

Even after the Oakland School Board revised its resolution (the second version clarified its intention to teach *teachers* skills in Black English), black critics persisted in denigrating Black English as a pedagogical tool. Why? Because the resolution makes blacks look laughable. Because Black English substitutes slang for language skills. Because the resolution would prevent black children from learning standard English, whatever that is. Because black folk had mastered standard English for so long that to acknowledge the validity of Black English would be to take a major step back for black kids. According to these critics, it is as if to acknowledge Black English is to somehow willy-nilly surrender the ability to speak standard English; and, perhaps most threatening, it is to suggest that *all* black folk speak Black English.

Well, as one white man who appreciated Black English said a few decades ago, "it ain't necessarily so." As to whether or not blacks are laughable, well, that's too subjective a judgment, too arbitrary a call. A lot of white folk have been laughing at black folk for a long time, especially when what black folk were doing was serious, threatening, or simply contrary to what they felt we should be doing. As to the charge that Black English wants to palm off slang as serious language, nothing could be further from the truth. Black English is not captured in slang like "yo" and "whassup," but in the use of the habitual "be," i.e., "she be singing" (Black English) as opposed to "she is singing" (standard English) and in the use of zero copulas (copulas in standard English use a part of "to be"), i.e., "he good" (Black English) as opposed to "he is good" (standard English).

It is equally silly to suggest that teaching teachers how to identify, read, and speak Black English will somehow promote greater illiteracy among black kids. The purpose of the resolution is to help teachers facilitate a transition from poor black children's primary, or home, language to so-called standard English. (Of course, if we tell the British that we Americans are speaking the King's English to the Queen's taste, they'd fall over laughing). What is the horror of recognizing that black kids, especially those from disadvantaged communities, speak a rule-governed, grammatically complex, syntactically consistent variety of English that, while it may be *different*, is not *deficient*. If a teacher is teaching American children French, it is a great boon if he or she knows English as well, to help out with grammatical errors and infelicities of style. There's no moral condemnation there; neither should there be with teachers learning Black English in order to better teach black kids so-called standard English.

The fact that figures like Frederick Douglass and Martin Luther King, Jr., were masters of so-called standard English doesn't mean that they were not equally in control of Black English. These men, like all great black rhetoricians, understood the value and virtue of what linguists and sociologists call "code-switching," or knowing when to speak so-called standard English and when to speak Black English. It's no insult to suggest that most black folk speak Black English; they do. Of course, most of us don't speak the stereotypical, hence wrongheaded, version of Black English that is a largely illusory concoction of dim-witted, mean-spirited hacks. But most black folk, even professional blacks, were reared in homes where family members reveled in the rich cadences, colorful imagery, profound metaphors, elegant stylings, and wonderful grammar of a people whose language was shaped by an imperative to define our identities as well as to defend our humanity.

The real tragedy of the black hysteria around Black English is that it is a sure index of the unruly pockets of self-hatred that persist in the collective black psyche. It is equally tragic that so many black critics of the Oakland School Board resolution deemed themselves sufficiently informed on such a complex topic as Black English, defiantly dismissing the work of sophisticated scholars who've spent their lives attending to such matters. It is perhaps the height of internalized racist ideology that we black folks believe that simply because we're black, we don't have to study our own culture, don't have to defamiliarize ourselves with what we take for granted in order to see the real complexity of what has shaped our lives.

Truth be told, perhaps we'd all benefit from remembering George Orwell's great essay "Politics and the English Language." Orwell writes that the defense of the English language has "nothing to do ... with the setting up of a 'standard English' which must never be departed from." Orwell writes that it "has nothing to do with correct grammar and syntax, which are of no importance so long as one makes one's meaning clear." Orwell contended that the real harm to the English language was "political writing," which consists "largely of euphemism, question-begging and sheer cloudy vagueness." Orwell said that the "great enemy of clear language is insincerity." He believed that when "the general atmosphere is bad, language must suffer."

We should heed Orwell's words in the discussions of Black English. The grim naysayers of black potential are the ones whose language is most opprobrious. Those folk who denigrate Black English without trying to understand it speak in bad faith. Those political critics who obfuscate their role in the economic suffering of the black ghetto with political chicanery are the real trouble. And those financially secure black folk who demean the users of Black English without working to get them better jobs, or to make sure that the future of the country's poorest black children is as bright as their own children's, speak a language of moral hypocrisy. If all of this is standard, then perhaps we should give non-standard a try.

Michael Eric Dyson
June 1997

Acknowledgments

I'd like to thank my wonderful editor at Addison-Wesley, Liz Maguire, without whose brilliance, insight, sharp analysis, and timely questions this book would not be! She shares, and supports, my intellectual and spiritual vision of the world. (Love ya, Liz.) I'd also like to express profound thanks to Mark Corsey, a very gifted editor and jack of all literary trades whose close reading of this book has made it stronger and tighter. I also thank Tracey George for her expertise and sweet spirit, brother Albert DePetrillo for his kindness, and the A-W staff for their tremendous support. I want to thank as well my supportive colleagues at UNC Chapel Hill's Department of Communication Studies. Y'all have been great!

I'd also like to thank my mother, Addie Dyson, and my nieces Brianna, KaTasha, Toccaira, Kayla, Charmaine and Brittany, and my nephew Everett, for all your love and support. I'd also like to thank my in-laws, Rosa and Dr. Matthew Smith, for your love and encouragement. And to my children, Mike II, Maisha, Mwata, and Jennifer (welcome to the family), thank you all for your love and encouragement.

I'd like to thank my beautiful, brilliant teacher Lola Black, who taught me French and gave me love and a sense of my worth as a budding scholar and intellectual. I'd also like to thank my other teachers: Mrs. Jefferson, Mrs. Harvey, Mrs. Morris, Mrs. Reed, Mrs. Stewart, Mrs. Click (to whom I owe great love and gratitude), Mr. Ewing, Mr. Cleveland, Mrs. Sutton, Mrs. Ray, Mr. Rogers, Mr. Jellife, Mr. and Mrs. Dagbovie, Mr. Low, and the lovely, talented Jewell Rogers.

I'd like to thank Dr. William Epps, Rev. Gerald Adams, and Rev. R. Michael Winters and Second Baptist Church, LA; Dr. Frank Thomas and New Faith Baptist Church, Matteson, Illinois; Dr. Joseph Roberts and Ebenezer Baptist Church,

Atlanta; and Dr. Henry Williamson and Carter Temple CME Church, Chicago, for their support, love, and inspiration. I'd also like to thank Leo and Cindy Rosenberg, for their precious friendship, extraordinary love, and incredible support. And I'd like to thank Laura Murphy, Madeleine Rabb, and your entire family for your extraordinary love, support, and generosity to me. I love you madly.

I want to thank as well my precious sister and brother, Joann Mitchell and Bob Bright. Your love and support have meant more to me than you can ever know. I love you with all my heart. I'd also like to thank my beautiful, wonderful, dear, dear friend, Sharon Elaine Kirkland, whose empathy, counseling, love—and pork chops—have nurtured me for many years. To D. Soyini Madison, my precious, precious friend, brilliant colleague, seer, mystic, and hermit, too, thanks for your expert reading and criticism of this book. I'd also like to thank my wonderful, special friend Danny Howard (and Nenaji) for his love and tremendous support. And I'd like to thank our extraordinary friends Rick and C.T. Powell for their matchless love, sweet spirits, and soul-saving friendship.

And finally, but certainly not least, I want to thank Marcia Louise Dyson, my wonderful, lovely, and long-suffering (!!!) wife. Thanks for putting up with my crankiness, grouchiness, and long, long hours in the study while I completed this book. Without you, this book couldn't have been done. Period. I love you.

Index